THE " JESUS FAMILY " IN COMMUNIST CHINA

THE Christian faith has constantly belied its critics by flourishing best in seemingly impossible circumstances. This thrilling story of how apparently unlettered peasants set out to follow quite simply, but quite deliberately, the pattern of the early church is a challenge to us of the western world to see if our complexities of life have rendered ineffective the essential spirit of our Christian profession; it is also a constant encouragement to see how fully the Christian simplicities triumph in the most unpromising conditions. And although since these words were written, many of the kindly *Yesu Chia-Ting*—"the Jesus Family"—have sealed their witness in blood and many more are in Communist prisons, still the light shines in darkness, and the darkness cannot put it out.

DR. D. VAUGHAN REES

THE " JESUS FAMILY " IN COMMUNIST CHINA

*A Modern Miracle of
New Testament Christianity*

*With twelve illustrations
by a Chinese Artist*

CHRISTIAN LITERATURE CRUSADE

FORT WASHINGTON   PENNSYLVANIA 19034

SPECIAL EDITION FOR WHITAKER BOOKS

89 SBN: 87508 463 X

Copyright © 1959 The Paternoster Press

This American Edition is published by arrangement with the Paternoster Press, Paternoster House, 3 Mount Radford Crescent, EXETER, Devon.

This Edition 1971

CHRISTIAN LITERATURE CRUSADE

CANADA
1440 Mackay Street, Montreal, Quebec

GREAT BRITAIN
The Dean, Alresford, Hampshire

AUSTRALIA
P.O. Box 91, Pennant Hills, N.S.W. 2120

NEW ZEALAND
Box 1688, Auckland, C.1

Also in:

Europe - Africa - South America - India
Philippines - Thailand - New Guinea
Pakistan - Indonesia - Japan
Caribbean Area

Made and printed in Great Britain

Contents

Introduction

NATIVE PEOPLES SUFFER BY CONTACT WITH US. WE over-awe them by certain superiorities, which they recognize immediately. We have no ground for boasting. These superiorities are products of the Gospel, products of what our Lord calls " salt " working in our midst. Even ungodly businessmen and traders have these qualities. All unknown to them, they have acquired them simply by contacts which allow them to draw on our spiritual capital. Basically, there is no difference between us and the native peoples. Native or white we are all sinners and " lost." It is not our superior intelligence or brains which have procured for us what we have, but the Fountain of Morality from which we have drunk. What a native lacks is not brains but integrity, and this can come only from the Lord and Giver of life, through the Gospel.

Therefore we missionaries need to be careful, or we shall produce native Christians who have lost their individuality. This is no theory, but a melancholy fact, known and seen by many. By contact with us, a native becomes one of our church members, if he is weak. If he is strong, he branches out for himself, as he should do, and becomes " anti-foreign."

Many of the indigenous movements, which have been called " anti-foreign," have been seriously misjudged. Missionaries have often found, when they have come into close contact with these movements, that they contain very excellent and beloved brethren in the Lord. They have pointed out our faults. We missionaries have faults, and often we have not had grace enough to confess and repent.

Finance, which is scarcely mentioned in the Acts of the Apostles, has today become a major issue. Because of the weakness of human nature, he who controls the purse-strings controls the power, and it is not the power of the Holy Spirit.

How many of us have said when funds were low, that the stringency proved that God had a controversy with us? Should we not rather have praised Him that He had cut down the source of our worldly power?

A native should never be denationalized; eventually, if we give the Holy Spirit time to work, he becomes super-nationalized.

This little book is an attempt to show the opportunity we missionaries have of giving " the more earnest heed " to the restraint of our overmastering personalities. The folk I mention here have overmastering personalities too. But they are subdued, as the account shows, in Christ.

They are all most precious and very beloved, tributes to the grace of God, and monuments, whether direct or indirect, to the power of the missionary movement in China. I waited more than two years before publishing these details for the first time. Then I felt free to do so, as those concerned would not have been made to suffer any more deeply than they are suffering at present.

Most of this book describes experiences between 1947 and 1949. At the end of the latter year I had to leave China. Since then, although the witness has been loyally continued, the lot of Christian groups refusing to toe the Communist party line has become progressively more difficult. But so soundly has the group about which I write learnt the principles of Christ, that persecution has not extinguished the light, and they are able to carry on their faithful witness in small groups and " household churches ".

THE HEATHEN MIND

In view of my remarks at the beginning of this introduction, it may be well to give some general illustrations of the way the heathen mind works.

Young men and women before going to the mission-field should know the forces arrayed against them. The heathen is not neutral, he is anti-Christian. A group of young Indian men, with whom I had become acquainted on the ship, urged me that on our arrival in Bombay I should visit a certain Hindu temple, because there they had special anti-Christian literature written for such a one as I. "But why should I read anti-Christian literature?" I asked.

"It will turn you from Christ," was the answer given with much emphasis.

"But why should I be turned from Christ? He has done me nothing but good."

A few days ago a young man and I were discussing Kipling's statement: "East is East and West is West, and never the twain shall meet". He asked me why it should be so. I found myself answering him by giving the following illustrations:

"A wounded Chinese general had been brought to my hospital for treatment. During my ward rounds we frequently chatted. One day we broached the subject of Western science. The general, who had had a Western education, said,

'You Westerners have an advantage over us Orientals in that you pool your knowledge and pass it on to others. But we also have a very deep knowledge, which we keep locked in families.'

"He then gave me this illustration of their 'very deep knowledge'.

"'One of my brothers was an official in Chinese Turkestan and there he became ill and died. You know our Chinese desire is to be buried with our ancestors. My brother's last wish was that his body should be taken home for burial. This entailed a journey of over a thousand miles by a dozen men carrying his coffin, a very difficult and expensive undertaking. Our family eventually decided to engage a necromancer whose knowledge had been handed down from generation to generation in his family. He was sent by us to

Turkestan, whence by his magic arts he walked my brother's corpse home by easy stages. When he arrived, we had the usual mourning ceremonies and safely buried my brother in the family tomb.' He then added triumphantly, ' Now that is something Western science couldn't do!' "

" Can this be proved?" broke in my young friend.

" My point is not the truth or otherwise of what the general said," I replied, " but the fact that he could tell it me in all good faith, in spite of his foreign education. This is the heathen mind. Now let me give you another example.

" I was on my way home. Between Singapore and Ceylon I became friendly with a young Indian journalist, an Oxford graduate, who was going back to England for further study. When the ship was moving out of Colombo, we were standing on deck together.

" ' Did you see me bidding my uncle good-bye?' he asked me. ' No,' I replied. ' I only tell you this because you have been so long in the East and understand,' he said, ' my uncle by the separation of his soul and body had come from Bombay in a moment of time to say good-bye. He is already back in Bombay, long before this.'

" Again his thought was that this was something that Eastern wisdom could accomplish which was impossible to science."

My companion again showed his amazement and incredulity. " How can it be proved?"

My reply was the same. " This is the heathen mind. Don't waste your time trying to prove or disprove these things; just be satisfied to know that this is the gulf that separates our thoughts from the thoughts of the heathen. The education of the heathen mind makes very little difference to it. You possibly have not read the long controversy in *The British Medical Journal* on ' Fire Walking ' (that is walking in a fire pit on hot stones), or the correspondence in *The Times* on the Indian rope trick. Weeks of correspondence and controversy by learned and experienced men produced nothing either constructive or conclusive."

As Christians we must accept the fact that this is part and

parcel of the darkness that envelops the East. This is the antithesis of the light and truth of the Gospel, which is the fountain from which our whole nation has drunk. In these days we like to think and talk of our progress, of our improvement, of the ancient superstitions and primitive mind, which the modern world has outgrown. Let me quote from Werner Keller's *The Bible as History* (p.80):

" In the twenties remarkable sherds were found on the Nile, the chief finds being at Thebes and Saqqara. Under the careful hands of experts the fragments were reassembled into vases and statuettes, but the most astonishing thing about them was the inscriptions they contained. The writing is full of menacing curses and maledictions. In accordance with an old superstition it was believed that at the moment the vase was smashed the power of the person cursed would be broken." These vases date from the 18th and 19th centuries B.C., nearly 4,000 years ago.

Does this belief belong only to what moderns delight to call " the primitive mind "? Let this example answer the question.

Last December my colleague, a foreign-trained lady doctor, came into the surgery looking distressed.

" I have just beaten my son, Hsien-Kang," she said—Hsien-kang is a boy of about nine years old.

" Why?" I asked, with a great deal of sympathy but not much interest.

" Because he broke a basin," she answered.

" Surely a small thing to beat him for," I said, surprised.

" I'm afraid I can't explain," she said, " because you Westerners do not understand; our worst curses against another are passed on by such means."

And so from her lips I heard the whole grisly story of her son's quarrel with a playmate, and his being encouraged to take this revenge by one of the servants.

This is not primitive, but still in this day and generation comes from the deceiver of our first parents. It encroaches on our land again in the form of Spiritism, Theosophy, Christian Science and other cults which exploit the so called

"Wisdom of the East", to our shame and degradation. It is because of this that we missionaries are so confident that we are on the right track. Only the Gospel and the Gospel alone will break the chains that bind China and the East.

Chapter One

MaChuang and the Ye-Su Chia-ting

WHEN COMMUNIST PRESSURE FORCED THE CHINA INLAND Mission hospital at Kaifeng in Honan to close early in 1948, the leaders of the Ye-Su Chia-ting—the Home, or Family, of Jesus—asked me to go North to Shantung province, to their centre, MaChuang. They wanted me to attend some wounded who had been gathered under their care.

We evacuated from Kaifeng and flew to Shanghai. In the company of Heng-shin, one of the leaders of the Ye-Su Chia-ting, I then went North to MaChuang, the centre of this indigenous movement. While I was there attending to the wounded, the Bamboo Curtain came down, and I was compelled to stay there for nearly two years. If the account I give here of my experiences seems too perfect an account of weak human nature, then you must magnify the grace of God in them. I can scarcely say less than I am about to say. I would not withdraw any of it, or say anything else than that this is an inadequate account of a most exceptional and enthralling experience.

This Christian centre, by God's providence, was prepared for by the present leader's great-grandfather more than one hundred years ago, although, as a pagan he had no knowledge that he was carrying out God's purposes. At that time, when a Chinese wished to sell a field, he placed a wooden stake in it, with an intimation to that effect written thereon. Anyone who picked up that piece of wood indicated by so doing his intention of buying the field.

The great-grandfather of Mr. Ching, the present leader, who was apparently very poor, was returning across the fields to his home one evening. Night was coming on, and in the dusk he stumbled over a piece of wood. Firewood was scarce, so he picked it up and carried it home. As he could not read the characters, he did not realize it was an offer of sale.

Next day the owner of the field traced his piece of wood to Mr. Ching's great-grandfather, who was much perturbed to find himself liable for the piece of land. Chinese custom held him fast, and he had to scrape together enough money to pay the bill. That piece of land passed down through four generations and is now the headquarters of the Ye-Su Chia-ting. It was about three acres but through additions has now grown to its present size of forty to fifty acres and supports about five hundred people.

My journey with Heng-shin to MaChuang lay through scores of country villages so squalid that they are really beyond the conception of folk at home. It was a region in which trees were not plentiful, and my attention was attracted by a line of unusually fine trees in the distance. Through a gap I could see the roof of a large building. Heng-shin pointed to it and said, " That's our chapel!" He passed the time during the rest of our slow journey across the plain telling me incidents in its building. Local workmen could not cope with many of the problems involved in erecting a building capable of seating a thousand people. The roof was the biggest problem of them all. Chinese tiles are set in a matrix of lime and mud, spread about two inches thick on an enormous mat of woven bamboo. This mat was the problem. Try to imagine a stiff sail of sufficient size to cover a large church. It was all of one piece and woven without seam throughout.

A hundred or more workmen, supporting the huge mat on their shoulders, moved by word of command up a specially erected frame. There had to be no wind. But, to the consterna-tion of all, a wind sprang up when the workmen were only halfway up the frame. The heathen present gloated, the Christians feared and prayed. As anticipated and feared, the wind lifted the ungainly thing clear of the shoulders of its bearers. There was a gasp of dismay, followed immediately by a cry of joy. It had descended exactly in position on the frame of the church. Angel hands could not have done it better.

Conversation equally pleasant and informative whiled away the time until we reached a quagmire. "This bog has troubled the district beyond living memory," said Heng-shin. "We are planning to mend it." While I was staying at MaChuang the plan was carried out and the bog was spanned by the best stone bridge in the district. Our mules with their cart attached eventually managed to struggle through it.

Now we could see our destination more clearly; houses and buildings could be seen through the dense growth of trees. Suddenly a score or more children burst through them, determined to be the first to welcome us. It was a lovely sight; they sang and danced and skipped as they ran. Tears came into my eyes. What a contrast to the poverty and squalor of the villages we had been passing through that day! I wondered at the variety and taste of their clothes. The grown-ups followed, walking in groups slowly and decorously as only Chinese do. They were all dressed poorly; no one dare do otherwise in Communist China. Their children's clothes were the outlet for their love of the beautiful. No greater contrast to them could be imagined than the filth, grime and rags of the village children we had seen on our way.

We entered the village through the dense barrier of trees. What heavenly wisdom their planting twenty or more years ago had been!

The Communists hate walls. Most of the villages and towns in China were walled, but now most of these old defences have been removed, often with dynamite and gun-fire. There must be no secrecy and no privacy, the Communists say, but their promise to prevent robbery has not materialized, " Freedom from poverty will do away with sin " was their slogan.

The Christian villages need privacy, and they need protection. Who but God knew that only trees would do for this? So years ago, at the inception of the work, trees were planted very closely in a broad belt all around the village. They grew slowly and almost unnoticed. Now they formed an impenetrable wall, with some of the trunks a foot across. Immediately the Communists came to power, they made the felling of trees illegal—this was part of their new agrarian policy—and so no zealous official dare touch these.

The gateway into the village is a gap in the trees. The houses and gardens of the enclosure cannot be seen from the outside. Only the church roof can be seen through a gap where some of the trees have died.

The cleanliness, order and apparent wealth of the community make all this necessary. It looks like one of the well-ordered foreign compounds once so common in China.

I could not help remembering Wesley's lament over his poor converts. "How can I prevent those lately converted to Christ from becoming wealthy? The wasteful become frugal, diligence replaces sloth, and the loveless becomes loving. How can such people remain poor or indigent?" So it is in China, and this is one of the problems of the Homes of Jesus.

"We cannot make all the improvements we would wish," said Mr. Ching to me one day. "As it is, the surrounding villagers are jealous of the progress we have made, and some of them would destroy us, if they could. Imagine if the passers-by could see freely into our compound! Their cupidity would be aroused at once."

Foreign pigs and a modern pigsty, a big Hereford bull and milch cows immediately met my eyes as we entered through the wall of trees. In Chinese villages glass is a rare curiosity. Here it is used in all the fowl houses. Electricity in China is unknown except in the big towns. Here the rooms have electric light, and over the big central well is an electric pump.

In spite of the shelter of the wall of trees all their best machinery is hidden in the most unexpected places, hidden from prying and jealous Communist eyes. As each new improvement was made, it was carefully camouflaged. The Communists are not the only ones who are adepts at conducted tours. While I was with them, these Christians showed the Communists only what they wished them to see, and invariably only the second-best was shown. They felt no need of window-dressing, a practice so common behind the Iron Curtain.

It was Heng-shin's job to conduct the sightseeing Communists around. There were many things and places they never saw. They were never taken into the machine-shop; I saw them being led past it on several occasions, when I chanced to be there.

On one occasion they were being conducted under the trellised vines, and it was obvious that they were very interested in the hanging bunches of grapes. Suddenly one of them said to Heng-shin, "How do you prevent your people from stealing the grapes?" They had made stealing on their communal farms punishable by death, and yet stealing went on. The question was pressed, "How do you stop it?" It was obvious to them that stealing was a thing of the past here, for there were the luscious bunches hanging as evidence.

Heng-shin answered simply that if anyone had the Lord Jesus in his heart, then he would not steal.

The tomtit, so the Chinese say, builds a secondary nest to deceive the cuckoo. These Christians had learned from nature's book and were always conspicuous in the secondary and less important places when the Communists arrived. I wondered when I was there, how much longer this would go on. Indeed, it was not long after my departure that the cupidity of the Communists got the better of them.

The Christians had a recognized birdcall which resounded all around the village when strangers arrived; their big dogs also gave tongue. (Believe it or not, they all believed that these dogs knew who was born again and who was not! Mr. Ching told me of one of their brethren from an outlying home who was dreadfully upset because the dogs had growled at him. "He confessed there was something wrong in his life and that he had grown lukewarm, and the dogs knew it.") Immediately on the warning note each took up his prearranged place unnoticed.

Only once during my stay did I see any group of Communists break through the atmosphere which seemed to surround and protect these people. The hand of God, the quiet dignity and confidence which pervaded this place, subdued even the most truculent. Why should God-hating men stand for ten minutes with bowed heads while grace was being said? And ten minutes was a short grace before meals by their normal standards. They all prayed aloud, each as he or she thought fit. The invited Communists sat at a separate table.

THE CHILDREN AT MACHUANG

The children's nurseries were a never-ending source of

wonder to the Communists. They gave their greatest interest
and closest attention to them. It was obvious that they
knew the importance of child indoctrination. I think what
amazed them was the strictness of the discipline, and the
responsive obedience and happiness of the children. Our
modern psychologists seem to think that self-expression is
a modern invention and sign of progress. No, the heathen
world has used it ever since it became heathen; that is one
of the marks of its heathenism. Why do the Chinese, on
becoming Christians, imediately reject self-expression for
themselves and their children? The children were a joy to
behold, and a testimony to the Communists above everything
else in these God-honouring communities. Astonishment sof-
tened the most outrageous Communist, when he saw these
little ones at mealtimes. In place of his own greed and dis-
order, each waited for the other. As each plate was filled, each
little one began to pray, and continued with its head bowed
and eyes closed until the last was served. Then chopsticks
or spoons were raised and the meal began. I have watched
a hundred children at prayer and failed to find a wandering
eye. I might mention four things that were novel to me:

1. There was a complete absence of toys and there were very few organized games.
2. The emphasis was placed by the teacher on singing.
3. The children were dedicated from their tenderest years to the deeper things of Christ.
4. The little boys and girls up to the age of six or seven all bathed in the open together.

In reading Wesley's *Journal* some years ago, I was particularly struck with the fact that there was no provision made for organized games among the children of his Kingswood schools. Remarkable indeed is it that I should meet the same system among these Christians in China, for none of them had read Wesley's *Journal*. They are producing the same fruit as Wesley produced; for it is a historical fact that Wesley remade England in the eighteenth century. This is a controversial point, especially in these days of such emphasis on sport.

The fact remains that I saw in MaChuang among these Chinese Christians perfectly happy, disciplined children, who seemed to have no need for ordinary physical culture and games. They turned work into play. They delighted in clearing up yards, gathering sticks, husking maize and carding wool, when they were not at their books. I watched them catching locusts and caterpillars; their teacher was with them, and a lesson in Biology was the result. When they were husking maize, I noticed that roast chestnuts were handed round. Some of the girls spun cotton with a distaff, some knitted. As far as I could see, there was always something for them to do; they were never idle.

Not infrequently I saw them, led by Helen Tso, engage in impromptu dancing on the threshing floor. Nothing is more delightful than to see children play and dance spontaneously. Games came naturally to these children, who bubbled over with joy. These children with their entirely natural way of life gave me a vision of The New Jerusalem, full of " boys and girls playing in the streets."

My next point is their singing. Have you ever heard children under ten years sing from the tonic sol-fa? Have you ever heard children younger than this sing " Cwm Rhondda " in three parts? In the evening under the willow trees a few chords on my mouth organ would bring the children in a body, ready for any well-known choruses (translated of course) and choruses of their own, until called to bed.

What to me were classical and difficult Chinese hymns, these children learned in a trice. Action songs were learned by little ones, who could scarcely toddle, and were sung on special days to a crowded chapel. Children from villages around were not forgotten, and on occasion were given the opportunity to show what they could do. As I observed it all, I could not but notice what a force for good this Christian community was, what an uplifting force, what " light " and " salt " to the district around. This is surely what Christianity does for us, this is the fountain from which we have drunk, and how often we do not recognize it. The worldling is a remittance man drawing on capital which is not his. Our civilization owes what it has to Christ Jesus.

Now we pass to my third observation. The children were dedicated to God from the beginning of their little lives. Our godparents mean little to us. It was not so with them; a real responsibility was assumed by them which was not easily cast aside.

" What are you going to be when you grow up?" I asked Chia-an, a little girl of four.

" I'm going to found a Home for Jesus, and be the Chia-Chang (Head of the Home)."

" Where?" I asked.

" In the United States!"

Next I asked a six-year-old boy, " And what are you going to be, Tao-chyen?"

" I'm going to be a preacher and preach Jesus."

" But how will you earn your living?"

" I shall be a stonemason."

Not one of these children had any other object in life than to preach Jesus, not only throughout China, but in all the world. The leaders of this movement are not at all afraid of what we call making the children lopsided. If ever there was a single eye to God's glory, it is here. "This one thing I do" is their watchword. Can it be wrong? From what I saw I am sure that it cannot. God will not let them down.

Go ahead, you dear Chinese Christians! I want to be like you. You have filled me with enthusiasm and thrilled me. You have shown me how needy I am.

The next point I made was the mixing of the sexes. This is regarded as wholly natural until the age of six, then separation is absolute until marriage. These people are made of the same stuff as you and I. I have listened to cases requiring disciplinary action, and I have listened to betrothals being discussed and marriages being arranged. How closely they approximate to Victorian ideals! Weak, effete human nature seems to need and even craves discipline. The male needs self-control; the female needs innocence and protection.

In their schools there was no such thing as education in matters of sex. The fear of God and obedience to His commands came first; matters of sex then fell naturally into their right relationship. The fear of God, they said, was the only safeguard, the one and only answer to the question of sex. Knowledge was no safeguard. Sexual education, in the nature of things, could not be timed aright. If given too early, it was not understood, and if too late what was the use of it? Innocence and the fear of God would save a maiden. Discipline, self-control, and fear of God were the safeguards of a man.

A childless marriage caused questioning, but large families were deplored. They considered that the love of husband and wife is first a matter of sexual attraction; later, husband and wife love because it is a command, "Husbands, love your wives." Thus they said, "We love one another as husband and wife because we are commanded to do so. Then remarkably, we find that it is so. Our love is then not the pawn of our passions."

THE ORGANIZATION OF A HOME OF JESUS

All of these Homes of Jesus had a basis of industry and farming which made them self-sufficient. But they were not concerned with industrial rights; they needed no other incentive than service. They looked on labour as a sacred trust, which was to be done for God. They had realized that not only is by far the largest part of mankind engaged in food production, but also that it is basic for all human life. So they seemed to have hit upon the right relationship of agriculture to industry and the arts and crafts.

First and foremost is agriculture. Is the idea of setting out to be an "industrial nation" not then basically unsound? They would say it is. Since labour is a sacred trust, to do one's best is to add interest and zest to one's work. The sanctity of labour is sufficient incentive. There was no need for such artificialities as five-year plans, production drives, and forty-hour weeks.

The centre of one of these Homes of Jesus was the chapel with its elders, pastors, and deacons. This was the apex of the pyramid. The base was, as I have said, agriculture. Then upon this was built various departments, which in Ma-Chuang were carpentry, bootmaking, bakery, smithy, machine shop and electrical department, stone masonry, schools and kindergarten, outside relations' department, financial department, printing, and bookbinding.

In MaChuang their livestock consisted of horses, mules, one blind donkey, cattle, pigs, geese, fowls, ducks and rabbits. The kitchens were large and well arranged, and all the utensils were made and cast in the blacksmith's department, even the large steam pressure cooker.

PRAYER AND WORSHIP AT MACHUANG

The chapel was the centre of their life of busy activity. Prayer always came first. Everyone went straight from bed to the chapel at 4 a.m.; each began to pray aloud as soon as he or she arrived; the hubbub was indescribable. This praying in unison is normal for all their times of prayer.

Our training and background make praying in unison confusing but it is not so with them. One only has to see a Chinese school, where every scholar shouts his lesson in his own way and time, to understand the difference. This method has much to commend it, for the timid are encouraged, thoughts become definite, and petitions concrete.

At about 5 a.m. there was normally a break for an address or testimonies. There followed "the morning watch," another period for prayer, which might continue until 8 a.m., when breakfast was taken. After that the day's work began.

The leaders prayed again at 9 a.m. and I used to join them. The meals were often seasons of prayer. Grace might take a quarter of an hour. Each department began its particular session with prayer, and as usual everyone in it prayed aloud in unison. Usually someone in the audience, or perhaps a leader, summed up by praying alone, and that ended the prayer session.

Will such a routine become monotonous? I did not find it so and the others did not seem to either. Everybody seemed refreshed. After the day's work, everyone gathered in the chapel, and the day's recreation and entertainment began. Prayer was again much in evidence. I asked one of the leaders if it were not confusing, when all prayed together. He looked surprised at my question, and then asked, "Confusing to whom?" I did not reply! Once again I found how wise and to the point many of their replies were. This was markedly so when they were dealing with truculent Communists. The church had been used all day as a place of work, and so the ropemaking and weaving which had been commenced there in the morning might continue right on through the evening meeting. The Communists, I might say, found no fault with this, and it was one of the many points in which their moves were anticipated.

Daily life and work in MaChuang was shot through with the sound of singing. The hymns were an expression of the zest Communist planning could never produce and were for the most part an expression of their experiences. I used to make a daily round of the departments and my interest was particularly aroused by their theme songs written on the blackboard in each department. These were modified or added to, until at last the complete product was printed in preparation for the hymnbook.

Their daily thoughts, their aphorisms and their struggles, all have a place in these hymns. The *Encyclopedia Britannica* says that there are more than half a million hymns in English. Here we see, in miniature, the powerhouse by which such a volume of praise, aspiration, and prayer is initiated and maintained. Groups of ordinary folk in China, who like us have been filled with enthusiasm from on high, sing their praise of Him who died for them. Mr. Fraser of Yunnan once said to me, " Music is the language of Heaven." So it is. " When I have Jesus, my heart bursts into song;" they say, " how can we keep from singing?" Hearts that had forgotten how to sing have learned the secret again.

I want now to describe a special evening meeting, which has stayed in my memory.

The lighting was good; all were at work, and one of the senior members was on the platform. There was to be prize-giving, I was told, so sweetmeats had been prepared, and various types of fruits, nuts, and small cakes, beloved by the Chinese. These were eaten as the meeting proceeded. Several hymns and psalms were sung, all without books. This, the normal procedure, used to try me a good deal, since, although I had a book, no numbers would be given out. My neighbours used to help me. " This is No. 57," someone would whisper. " That is Psalm 39." Most of the hymns had tunes composed by the Chinese, but there were also translations of some of the greatest English hymns, for example that glorious one by Charles Wesley : " And can it be that I should gain an interest in my Saviour's blood?" They had a marvellous aptitude for putting the Psalms to metre, and the result reminded me of the Scotch psalmody. Nearly all they sang they knew by heart.

Prayer then began and went on for some time, until all the prayers seemed to be summed up in one, and that one closed the prayer time.

The chairman then asked all the old men over seventy to come to the front seats. He announced that after they had received their prizes there would be testimonies by visitors from outlying Homes. Someone whispered to me that there were Communists present in the meeting.

" Tonight's prize-giving is unique," said the chairman. " During the summer months the blow-flies have been very bad. Each of our older brethren was given a fly swatter and asked to keep a record of the number he killed. Prizes are to be given to the first three."

The old men now stood and gave out their numbers. I was apparently not the only one surprised at the large numbers given, for suddenly a Communist got up and said, " Surely you cannot believe what they say. How do you know they are telling the truth?"

Obviously the numbers were true, for none took advantage of the other. And what amazed the Reds was that everyone seemed to believe what they said. In private conversation afterward, the Communists further expressed their amazement, and admitted that such a scene would have been impossible in their own meetings. Again we had the same old question, " How do you make people tell the truth?" This question took on new significance when I came to know more about Communist " brain washing." Their technique is devilish psychological torture. How had these Christians done it?

The chairman then gave a short talk on " Christ the Life and Christ the Truth." " Truth is a Person," he said. After this the testimonies began; there were sixteen in all. Each one who testified was given *carte blanche* as to the time he or she spoke.

The Chinese are tireless in matters like this. The meeting began at 5 p.m., the testimonies at 8.30. I left for bed at 2 a.m. The meeting ended at daybreak. Everyone was refreshed and had a thoroughly enjoyable time, though obviously the normal routine was not followed the next day. I cannot remember whether this held the record for long meetings. The Chinese are good trenchermen where meetings are concerned, and " eat " long and enthusiastically.

Sleep did not take long to " bind up the ravelled sleeve of care," but my last thought was of the truth-telling old men, and their testimony to the Communists.

I cannot close this section without telling something of their meal-times. It was at these that I met many of the leaders of outlying churches and homes.

"This is Mr. Hwang from East Village," said Mr. Ching, introducing him. "He was converted last year and has now started a church in his village." I looked at Mr. Hwang. He was obviously an illiterate country man. We shook hands; he had the knotted hands of a farmer. "And this is Mr. Liu," continued Mr. Ching. Obviously Mr. Liu was an educated man. "He is the headman of their village," I said to myself, for he came from the same village as Mr. Hwang.

"Mr. Hwang saved Mr. Liu's life," said Mr. Ching. Again I found myself thinking that it was probably a case of a farmer willing to sacrifice his life for his landlord, something not uncommon in old China.

The facts proved to be otherwise. After the church was founded by Mr. Hwang, Mr. Liu, the scholar, joined. Their church offended the Communists in some way. All the members were marched out and Mr. Liu was chosen to be shot. "But he is not the leader, I am," said Mr. Hwang, "therefore I am the one to be shot." He continued to claim his right as he followed the group to the place of execution. The Communist officer laughed at Mr. Hwang's dialect. A laugh in China means much. This one meant that Mr. Liu came back from the jaws of death and was freed. On such trifles hang the issues of life and death.

What a season of delight meal-times were! Everybody was so happy and enthusiastic. I was always given an honoured place though I did not deserve it, and in everything I was dependent on them, a true "rice Christian", if ever there was one. The boot was now on the other foot, and how they appreciated it! It was gratifying to me, too. No more could I be taunted with making "rice Christians" in China, for I was now one! This was indeed a restoration of their "*amour propre*," that "face" which is so dear to the Chinese.

I remember the oft-repeated words of Mr. Hoste, of beloved memory: "Remember, Doctor, the Chinese are an imperial people."

With Mr. Ching, everything Chinese was best. Their food was the best, their history was the longest and their women made the best wives. It followed therefore that there was no foreign flavour in their Christianity. It was theirs and was exclusively Chinese in every way. How wonderful is Christianity that it can thus adapt itself!

Mr. Ching and I clashed occasionally, but seldom seriously. The following incident was not serious. We were eating cobs of maize. "Try some butter on it and a little salt, that is the way we eat it," I said.

"We Chinese like the natural flavour, we do not like to cover it with anything else," was his reply.

The next day we were eating cucumber; the Chinese like sesame seeds with cucumber, so I waited my chance. "Try some sesame on it," said Mr. Ching, passing the seeds. He had forgotten the passage of arms of the previous day.

I was ready and replied, "We British like the natural flavour, we do not like to cover it up." There was a roar of delighted appreciation at my hit.

Besides all this, meal-times were also a time of social intercourse, and the time for taking stock of growth. The visitors were invited to sup, and there one learnt of new groups that had been formed, of new districts opened up. There one also learnt of the trials and sufferings of those undergoing persecution.

Mr. Chang sat down with us one day and was introduced to me as another who had been through the valley of the shadow of death. He walked with bowed back and a bad limp. He had been condemned by the Communists to be beaten to death.

He could give me very few details of his accusation and trial, chiefly because of his confusion of mind. The executioner, having tied him up and commenced the torture, stopped and said, "I am like Jesus, aren't I? For I have the power of life and death over you. If you admit that I am

Jesus, I will let you down."

Mr. Chang, in recounting his sufferings, said that, although he was scarcely conscious, he turned his head to his tormentor and said, " You are the Devil." This remark, spoken with almost his last breath, saved him. For the executioner was laughed out of countenance by the Communist soldiers standing around. He threw down his bamboo, and went off in a huff, leaving his victim hanging. One of the soldiers undid the thongs and Mr. Chang crawled away.

Chapter Two

The Leaders of the Ye-Su Chia-ting

THERE ARE FOUR SPIRITUAL LEADERS OF THE YE-SU CHIA-ting, two men and two women: Mr. Ching-tien-yin, Mr. Tung-heng-shin, Dr. Bessie Chen and Miss Helen Tso. One of the Chia-ting hymns has something to say about leadership. Here is a translation:

Love is the organizing principle of the Home of Jesus. This is a heavenly conception, and man had small part in its growth. Since we are fathers and sons by grace and brothers in the Spirit, leadership is weak and bodily life is very strong. All are "one in Christ," whether old or young, male or female, dull or gifted. All worldly differences are ignored, tribe or nation, rich or poor, honourable or lowly. Truly our aim is, "Thy kingdom come, Thy will on earth be done."

I experienced the truth of the line, "Leadership is weak and bodily life is very strong." Mr. Ching, though he is the founder of the movement and a recognized spiritual leader, was not the leader where the authorities were concerned. During the two years I was in MaChuang Mr. Chow-shin-ming was the leader in this respect, and Mr. Chuin-hsaing was his assistant.

MR. CHING-TIEN-YIN

Mr. Ching was born in Shantung about the year 1890 and was given the name Tien-yin. His early life was spent under the tutelage of his father, who was a Chinese medical practitioner and an ardent Confucianist. Confucianists have a misty knowledge of one true God, whom they call Shang-Ti.

When the boy Tien-yin was about eight or nine years old, he made a vow to Shang-Ti that he was determined to know him better. About the first year of the Republic (circ. 1910), he went to a Methodist school in Tai-an because there was no better school in the district. Both he and his father were opposed to Christianity. He was the oldest in his class. One day the teacher proposed that he should be their representative. He accepted. Then came the day when someone suggested that since he was the leader, he ought to be baptized. His Confucian principles of rectitude accepted this, and although he was still strongly opposed to Christianity he agreed.

Of all non-Christian religions Confucianism has produced the best civilization. Its ethics are better than those of Hinduism, Buddhism, or Mohammedanism, and there is none of the debasement of womanhood one finds in these religions. If, for instance, a Chinese takes a concubine, the first wife never loses her right or position. She is always the head of the household and the one respected and obeyed. Chinese women are the basis of Chinese life. Communism is ruining what was China's mainstay.

Young Tien-yin, having been baptized, was now in an equivocal position, which had to be clarified. The test was not long in coming, for workers were needed in a Methodist church function. Only Christians were eligible. Those in the class who were Christians were asked to stand. Young Tien-yin stood. The die was cast. He saw that he must believe in Jesus, or he was not " treading the path of rectitude," a phrase constantly used in the Confucian classics. Thus did Confucius become his schoolmaster to lead him to Christ, that he might be " justified by faith " (Gal. 3 : 24). He began to study the Bible closely, and in his testimony to the Communists he says, that as he read, he saw that Jesus was greater than Confucius and the only Saviour of the world, " for He died on the cross for my sins."

A further crisis in his life was now reached, for when he thought to know more of this Jesus and to follow Him, his conscience began to trouble him, for he was divorced. Several years before he had sent his wife back to her mother's home. " She had bound feet, and was not my equal, so I thought;

and I didn't love her," he told me once, when he was giving me an account of his early life. The next step in his eventful history was to find out what the Bible had to say about divorce. He turned to Ephesians 5: 25, and found, "Husband love your wives." He expected that the passage would add, "if they are pretty or clever or good." But no, there was the bald statement, and nothing more. He shut the Book, for it did not answer his difficulty in the way he wanted it to.

Next day he did the same thing, still half hoping and expecting to find the words he wanted. On several occasions he did this; and then finally he gave in. He dropped on his knees and prayed, "God, if you have commanded me to love my wife, I must be able to and I will." On his knees he promised that he would go to her village and bring her home the next day. Since she had bound feet, she could not walk the fifteen

miles to his home. It was necessary for him to find a conveyance. There was none available, not even a barrow. When he
told me this, he added that in later life he has always been
surprised that he didn't think to himself, "O God, now that I
have made such a sacrifice, and done such a big thing for
You, You might have made it easy for me and prepared a
barrow." But all he thought of was that he must keep his
promise.

After putting the situation to his wife he did an impossible
thing for a Chinese to do. He put her on his back and
carried her home. As soon as they entered the door of his
home together the Holy Spirit descended on them both.
This was in 1920. In 1940 I received a broken hearted
letter from him. His beloved wife was dead. She had proved
his equal and beloved companion for twenty years. Contrary
to his former opinion, she was the backbone of the work
which had started in 1921.

At that time Mr. Ching and his wife had sold all their pos-
sessions and had given them to the poor. With a few who
were likeminded he and his wife commenced a co-operative
store, then silk-weaving, and then a chapel was built on the
land he had given to the Lord. This formed the nucleus of
the work, and farming was commenced.

The piece of land which is the centre of this work was
the one which Mr. Ching's great-grandfather had had to buy.
It is so essentially suitable in every way, that it is clear that
God was preparing His vessel more than a hundred years
earlier.

During the early 30's, Mr. Ching and his companions took
evangelistic tours all over North China. In 1935, my wife and
I met them for the first time in South Kansu, more than a
thousand miles from where the work had first begun.

Repeatedly Mr. Ching said to me, "The China Inland Mis-
sion is our mother and father [as he expressed it in his
Chinese idiom]. It was from *The Life of Hudson Taylor*, by
Mrs. H. Taylor, in its Chinese translation that I received my
first stimulus to preach the Gospel to my fellow Chinese.
Here I caught a glimpse of what self-sacrifice really means."

MR. TUNG-HENG-SHIN

Mr. Ching's constant companion on his preaching tours was Mr. Tung-heng-shin. He was the Charles Wesley of the Home of Jesus. How marvellously God selects His workers! Without Heng-shin the work which Mr. Ching has done would scarcely have been possible. How can a church be formed without hymns? Under Heng-shin's leadership these Chinese churches were full of song, the sweetest singing imaginable. And so these two were the spiritual descendants of John and Charles Wesley, Moody and Sankey, Chapman and Alexander.

Have you ever heard of a church congregation at home singing the *Hallelujah Chorus* of Handel's *Messiah* in parts? At Christmas, 1948, Heng-shin was conducting the MaChuang choir when, just as they were about to sing the *Hallelujah Chorus*, he turned around to the congregation, divided them according to their voices into bass, tenor, alto, and soprano, and they sang the "Hallelujas" in parts.

I first found out Heng-shin's gifts by accident, one day when I was in an American hospital in Central China. While convalescing I was the doctor's guest; I was laboriously strumming out some birdcalls on the piano in his drawing-room. Some musical genius has set the wonderful songbirds of China to music.

Heng-shin was standing by, no doubt pained at my clumsy efforts. To my surprise he asked for a try. I did not then know what ability the Chinese had, as I knew it subsequently. All the birds of the Chinese bush and moorland came into that missionary drawing-room. Have you ever listened to a recording of birds in an English coppice? Chinese birds can be just as sweet. It was to Heng-shin that this Chinese indigenous church owed its ever-increasing stock of hymns. It is good to see that he is not alone in this, for song is breaking out from hearts that have been dumb for centuries.

Jazz and syncopation are no new thing; they killed music in China. (I have heard an old Chinese teacher, an M.A., deplore the fact that Chinese music is not what it was in

the time of Confucius. He knew this because Confucius was
a musician and wrote about music.) Heathen music is full of
jazz. These Chinese Christians will have none of it.

I often listened with delight to Heng-shin's rendering of
the *Magnificat*—his own composition. But he was not
always like this! Opium smuggling was once his occupation.
He was a constant traveller between Nanking and Shansi. He
substituted a smaller container for the usual large one in his
thermos flask. It was easy for him to fill the large cavity
left with opium. He went back and forth with impunity
and was never caught. If he had been it would have meant
his death—such was the penalty inflicted by General Yen-shi-
shan's government. He told me that he had repeatedly re-
proached himself for thus risking his life, but had never succeeded in stopping it until he became a Christian. Then
Christ stopped it for him.

After his conversion he became the leader of Governor
Yen's brass band. But Christ called, and he entered the Bap-
tist seminary in Kaifeng, where he became song leader. There
he met Mr. Ching and gave his life to the evangelization of
China.

The secret of the great change in his life, he told me, was
the filling of the Holy Spirit. That is doubtless the origin of
Heng-shin's wisdom in dealing with truculent Communists
and their questions.

He has been in gaol, and has been near death several times.
Gaol and death have been the lot of many of these Christian
brethren. He is thoroughly Chinese in thought, and is only
second to Mr. Ching in his knowledge of the Classics and the
ancient wisdom of China. These things the Communists now
despise. He frequently corrects the poor literary style of local
Communist documents, since he is in charge of all the outside
relationships.

When I was in Tsinan, and we were both standing in the
presence of a young Communist commissar, he utterly nonplussed those gathered around by correcting the dossier they
had made of my doings. He was dressed like a coolie, and they
naturally thought his mental accomplishments were in keep-

ing with his dress.

This wisdom of his replies filled me with admiration. The commissar spoke contemptuously of this "foreign religion," and asked how much the Ye-Su Chia-ting received from abroad. Heng-shin denied that there was any financial help or connexion whatever, but added, "There is a very close spiritual relationship. We love them and they love us."

Then he told the following story: "When you Communists were in charge of our district last year, some of your soldiers came to our village to buy vegetables. Planes flew over, and there was danger of their seeing us, so I asked the soldiers to take cover. 'Oh, they won't bomb you,' said the sergeant, 'those are English-American planes, and they know you are one of their churches.' I said nothing; what was the use?—for I knew that he would not believe. Some time later you were driven out, and I was arrested by the Nationalists for harbouring your soldiers. I was brought before their colonel on a capital charge. His secretary recognized me and said behind his hand, 'Say you are an English-American church and you will be let free immediately.' I said nothing. I was not executed, though for sometime it was threatened. The Lord intervened when my execution was imminent." The Communist was silent but I could see he was very impressed.

Sometime later Hing-shin was with me on Tai-shen Mountain, a desolate mountain which these people are transforming; I asked him about some big foundations. "Oh, those," he said, "those are of houses for tired missionaries to live in, when they come up here for a holiday." It was their intention to give holidays free of charge to tired or sick missionaries, but unfortunately these plans have fallen through. Nevertheless, "it was good that it was in thine heart."

DR. BESSIE CHEN

As leaders of the women's work God has raised up two ladies. The lives of these two are so interwoven that they can be scarcely separated.

They were both working in the Peking School of Midwifery

when the Lord called them. Dr. Chen was in the department of Obstetrics and Gynæcology, and Helen Tso was a teacher in the school. They were both accomplished young ladies, and were noted in the social life of Peking, especially in its dancing salons; both were prominent in skating and sport.

Dr. Bessie came from a wealthy Hankow family; both her mother's and father's families were Christians for two generations.

When she decided that she was going to study medicine, she was by no means a keen Christian; in fact, she doubted if she was even converted. An application for entry into the Peking Union Medical College was rejected on health grounds, although she had passed the entrance examination.

Hong Kong was her next thought, but for this she not only had to do her medical course in English, but also had to undergo the stiffest of competitive examinations. Of the several hundred candidates in Hankow she took first place, the only one who was admitted to the Hong Kong University from that city. Her mother's great hope was that she should do postgraduate work in Obstetrics and Gynæcology in England.

The Lord had other plans, and her medical work became a sideline to the women's evangelistic work she and Helen Tso conducted in many parts of China.

MISS HELEN TSO

Miss Helen Tso's ancestors on both sides had been officials under the Manchu dynasty. Her father was a man of such rectitude that in the era of corruption under the war-lords (1910-1930) the famous General Wu-pei-fu visited their home, after her father had retired in dismay, and personally begged him to take office again.

What she told me of her home life reminded me of the descriptions of the official Chinese home of the eighteenth century. (An excellent account of this period is given in *Hong-leo-meng*, a Chinese novel written just before Richardson, Fielding, Smollett, and others were writing the first novels in English, and written in much the same style.)

The members of her family, a large one, were all strict Confucianists. Her grandfather had warned them that should any of them become Christians, their names would be erased from the family register, and they themselves would be outcasts from the family clan, which was a serious matter for the ancestor-worshipping Chinese.

In spite of the family's attitude Helen was sent to a Presbyterian ladies' school, the most exclusive in Peking. It shows what value was placed on missionary schools. There she received a Christian training, the influence of which never left her. For some years she remained outwardly the same, until one night she was invited to a little mission hall in Peking. She and Bessie went together. Here they were both converted and, as she says, baptized in the Holy Spirit amid floods of tears, which at the time surprised her, and for which she could give no adequate explanation.

A revival spread through the school of Midwifery, and a group of young Chinese women, of whom Bessie and Helen were the leaders, banded themselves together to preach the Gospel and heal the sick in Mongolia. That young ladies of the calibre of this group should give up everything at the call of Christ was something new in Peking social and educational circles. Every obstacle that man's craft could devise was used to obstruct their going. A telegram from the Minister of Education in Nanking was sent to reinforce the pleading of their college superintendent. This having failed, lawyers were then employed to intimidate them, and the old Chinese pastor, who had been the means of their conversion, was put into prison on a false charge. There was a very big stir, and this old gentleman had to take the blame. At his trial, of course, nothing could be proved against him, and he was freed. He then voluteered to go with them to Mongolia, and eventually on the border of Inner Mongolia they established midwifery clinics. Having established their base, they then travelled far and wide, attending to needy women. They had much difficulty in obtaining a permanent building; for some time all that was available to them was half of a large building used as a brothel.

Then began the most difficult period of all. Their relatives began to arrive begging them to return. Nothing could describe the horror with which these relatives viewed the surroundings in which these girls were living and working for Christ's sake.

Church leaders from various parts of China followed, including one from Hong Kong, to see and persuade Dr. Bessie. "But the most difficult one to encounter of all those who came," said Miss Tso, in recounting their adventures to me, "was my own dear father. Little did I guess what the outcome would be," she added.

This proud Confucian official, her father, was so impressed by what he saw, that there and then began the work which in the end led him to give his heart to "Him who is greater than Confucius."

It was in this region that they met Mr. Ching and his companion, Mr. Tung, who were travelling up to the North-West to preach. The young women then divided; half went on with Mr. Ching, and half stayed to carry on the work in Inner Mongolia. Part of this journey took them through the Gobi desert.

In Ning-hsia the hand of one of the young ladies was sought by the brutal Moslem governor, Ma-pu-fang. Her refusal awoke his anger, and she even suffered imprisonment at his hands. There she contracted tuberculosis and eventually died. Helen and Bessie buried her not far from the place she had sought to evangelize. In 1934 they arrived in Lanchow, now Kaolan, in Kansu, and there for the first time my wife and I met Dr. Bessie, Helen and Heng-shin.

How glad I would be to write biographies of young women like these—of those who have laid down their lives, and those who are about to do so, in the cause of the evangelization of China and its women!

Dr. Bessie Chen's time is now fully occupied with medical duties among the mothers and children at the Homes of Jesus. But she finds time to do much translation from English into Chinese. Her literary Chinese finds much praise even from Mr. Ching, and he will pass nothing second rate. I watched them together translate, "Full Salvation," and some of Wesley's hymns, such as, "And can it be that I should gain an interest in the Saviour's blood?"

Miss Helen Tso's great ability and energy take her into every department of these Homes. Four months after I had applied for a Communist pass out of China, it was suddenly granted. When I originally made the application, I mentioned to Helen that I had no foreign clothes, and that if the Communists allowed me to go, I could scarcely go abroad in Chinese dress. She told me not to worry, took a tape out of her pocket and measured me. I asked her if she had ever made a foreign suit. The reply was, "No," but that she had some pictures from which she might be able to manage something.

I wasn't very sanguine. When the pass was granted, I suddenly thought of my clothes. My anxiety was unnecessary. The day before my departure Helen arranged all the necessary clothes for packing, three foreign suits and a foreign overcoat, with shirts and ties to match, also socks and shoes. Later I found a handkerchief of the right shade neatly placed into the breast pocket of the blue serge suit.

"What will the Communists say when they examine my baggage, and see all these fine suits?" I inquired. She replied that all the material had come from Chinese gowns, which had not been used for some years. Their owners had discarded them for poorer clothing on entering the Home of Jesus. The overcoat is a masterpiece; it is lined with astrakhan, and has a fur collar. It is rather too ornate to wear at home, as it also has an inside silk covering, similar to the best-tailored Chinese coats.

Chapter Three

The Communists Anticipated

Thou compassest my path and my lying down (Ps. 139: 3).
*Commit thy way unto the Lord; trust also in him; and he
shall bring it to pass* (Ps. 37: 5).
He led them forth by the right way (Ps. 107: 7).

MUCH THAT I HAVE TOLD IN THE PREVIOUS TWO CHAPTERS
suggests how the Ye-Su Chia-ting was being prepared
for the ordeal that lay ahead of them. When the crisis
of Communist rule came, they found in many ways that
Divine guidance had prepared them for the new circumstances, and that they had all-unknowingly anticipated many
of the Communists' main objections to Christianity in practice.
In this chapter I wish to show how the Lord was unmistak-
ably preparing their path. Their formative years were in the
20's. God's plan began to take shape in the 30's.

My wife and I first met them in the early 30's in the
extreme North-West province of China, called Kansu. I
stayed with them in MaChuang, their headquarters in the
North-Eastern province of Shantung, between 1947 and 1949.
At the end of my enforced stay it was thrilling to look back
as I said good-bye at the station some miles away. Mr. Ching
took my hand and said, "Little did I think, my brother, in
1930, how the Lord would lead, and what He had in store
for us. How foolish and ignorant I was. Now see what He
has done. He raised us up for this purpose, that the Communists might see what Christianity is."

Heng-shin and I squeezed into the crowded third-class com-
partment, the whistle blew and we parted, in all human pro-
bability not to meet again until we stand before our Lord,
theirs and ours. In Shanghai I soon had a Communist exit
permit, and embarked for Hong Kong.

As we sailed down the China coast a young Chinese refugee said to me: "Doesn't Christianity tell us to sell what we have and give to the poor? And Communism says much the same, when it condemns private ownership. Isn't that so?"

"Partly," was my reply, "but the great and fundamental difference is this. I can sell what I have and give to the poor, but I cannot force you to do it. If I were a Communist I could." The Chinese are clever and nimble-minded. Thus they saw immediately the question of the Communist use of force, and its ultimate end in dictatorship.

A Communist once said to me, "Dictatorship is necessary for the present, but our children and grandchildren will reap the benefits, for then dictatorship will have been swept away."

Nemesis has descended upon those who have "darkened counsel with words without knowledge." Quite apart from the very naïve attitude toward the lust for power that is inherent in human nature, this statement reminds of one that a noted rationalist used to make: "The Christians would put off our Heaven until the future; I want mine now." Where Communism has seized power and atheism rules, the folly of this has become apparent. There is no Heaven under Communist rule, except for the Christian, who by his peace shows that he already enjoys it although he waits for it in the future as well.

When I first had the opportunity of observing the Communists who came in groups to the compound, I noticed they were in a truculent fighting mood. Their attitude invariably was: "We will show these Christians what a true life of equality is. Among us there are no leaders, everyone is a comrade."

One day a typical group of them came and called loudly for the pastor. (They did not give him this title, but Chia-chang; this is often used and means Head of the House.) I saw him in the distance. He was pushing the manure cart, and he pushed it right into their midst before someone said, "Here he is." The Communists had drawn back from the offensive cart. They then wanted to know how he could keep adequate discipline, when he did such a menial job. (It is of course the lowest coolie's job.)

Chow-shin-ming, the pastor and official head of the community, explained that since they were all equal, he the leader had the privilege of doing the worst jobs. The Communists looked sheepish. They knew that their theories of equality were not working while here was an obvious demonstration that those of the Christians were. Where they had failed, the despised Christians had succeeded.

The Chinese Communists boast of their land tenure theories. "They are better than those of either Marx or Lenin; we are going to change the Russians," said a Peking professor of Chemistry to me. How have these Christians dealt with some of their land problems?

The most important thing is that anyone who wishes to be a leader among them must first have sold his land and given it to the poor, with all his other belongings.

I have yet to hear of a Communist who has done this, although I have heard of many who are not Communists who have. But this is something that has been forced on the landowners of China by torture and death. These Christians had done it before ever the Communists arrived. A Communist remarked on how fit they looked, robust and rosy-cheeked. He inferred that they ate well and therefore had large holdings of land. His questions followed, "How many acres have you? What is your food?"

Heng-shin was the one questioned and he replied "We have forty-three acres among five hundred people."

The Communist was amazed; "Less than one-tenth of an acre per person!" How could it be! He knew that only land culture and frugality of the highest order could manage on this. In Shantung the Communists allowed one acre per person as the minimum. They divided land into five categories for taxing, the average yield over several years fixing the grade. The Ye-Su Chia-ting paid no taxes, or did not up to 1950; it follows that their land must therefore have been of the lowest grade. This was an anomaly which may have been adjusted since, for though their area was low grade land, their yearly yield far exceeded the average.

"Fancy," said the local people, "they are so poor they don't pay taxes." Their food, though adequate, was greatly despised. "Copy the Chia-ting in everything but their food," was a local byword.

The Communists boast of their philanthropy, but it is a poor thing compared with Christian giving. This reminds me of a story that appeared in the *Nineteenth Century* magazine:

Huxley in a letter to Gladstone spoke slightingly of General Booth and the Salvation Army slum schemes:

"The slum schemes of the Rationalistic Association will be far better than anything that Booth and his Army can do," he said.

Nearly one hundred years have gone by. Where are the slum schemes of the Rationalistic Association?

The Communists have philanthropic schemes too. One was boasting of these while I was at MaChuang, and asked these Christians how much they gave away. "Nine-tenths of our produce," was the astounding reply.

This was too much for the Communist, and too much for me also! So at the first opportunity I drew Heng-shin aside and asked him, "What do you mean, when you said that this year you gave away nine-tenths?"

"It's like this," he said. "In 1930 we began to tithe; in this way we continued for over ten years. In 1942 there was a great famine, and there were so many starving people, that we felt we should add a tenth. The Lord so blessed us, that we felt the next year we could not stop there, and so every year since we have added a tenth; thus this year we are giving away nine-tenths."

I asked, "What have you been giving me to eat?"

"Just what the Lord sends you," was his reply. "You pray the Lord's Prayer, 'Give us this day our daily bread,' don't you?"

"So that's it," was all I could reply.

It was obvious that I was being carried along on the impetus gained from their faith. What can the Communists do with devotion such as this?

Since I left Red China I have received letters from both Miss Helen Tso and Dr. Bessie Chen. One sentence will suffice: "We thought we would have nothing to eat today, and only water to drink, but the Lord has been good to us and given us *hoodoo*" (gruel to which they add edible weeds).

The question arises, if their farming is so efficient, how can they be brought to this pass? They have learned the vitamin content and calorific value of most things that are edible, including for obvious reasons weeds and spring tree-shoots. And they have done this for the mysterious reason that they give away all they have. Amazing fact, this year they have tithed themselves up to ten-tenths of the produce of their farms!

"And He . . . saith unto them, Verily I say unto you, That this poor widow hath cast more in, than all they . . . for all they did cast in of their abundance; but she of her want did cast in all that she had, even all her living" (Mark 12: 43, 44).

Fellow-Christians, show me devotion like that and you have shown me something that will conquer the world. No more need for conferences on how to combat Communism!

I have just been reading through a brochure on Communism, which took a committee of a certain church two years to compile. I sit back and consider it, meditating. How mixed and confused are my reactions to it! Then I read that letter from Dr. Bessie Chen and I am thrilled. "O God, let me do something like that," I say instinctively, with my whole being aglow.

CHAPELS AND SUNDAY OBSERVANCE

The keeping of Sunday is particularly disliked by the Communists, and church buildings used only for worship are special objects of their scorn. Excuses are made for getting rid of both Sunday and the buildings. That the chapels of these indigenous groups have been preserved is truly a cause for astonishment, when one sees the destruction and destitution in village after village.

It is no wonder that a Roman Catholic priest said to me,

"Christianity in North China is finished. Chapels and cathedrals are in ruins, and congregations disbanded." He was incredulous when I assured him that I had just attended a conference at which there were more than seventy leaders of churches in Shantung alone.

The reason the Ye-Su Chia-ting chapels were allowed to stand is, first, because they have been used by the Communists for their meetings. In country districts there are no other buildings for their propaganda meetings, so by using them the Communists have tacitly admitted the right of the Christians to use them also. Next, so many of the chapels are nothing more than enlarged rooms in private houses. This reminds us of St. Paul's words in I Corinthians 16: 19, and elsewhere: "Aquila and Priscilla salute you . . . with the church that is in their house."

Very frequently a Chinese family, on becoming Christians, will adapt or alter a room in their house and gather in the neighbours. This becomes the nucleus and beginning of the church in that village. The Communists cannot destroy the church without destroying the home.

There is again a further point. For some years now the local churches of the Chia-ting have emphasized the sanctity of labour. To them work done in the name of the Lord is worship. Their chapels are therefore used as workshops, where weaving, spinning, sewing of shoes, and knitting are carried on. As soon as the service begins all noisy work is stopped. The zest for singing and testimonies is if anything enhanced by such a method. "Music while you work," becomes a very pleasant fact. This has given the Communists a shock. But on the other hand in such a crowded and poverty-stricken land, there is perhaps something to be said for the Communist point of view, that church buildings are a waste of space and building material.

Sunday is used by the Chia-ting churches as a day on which work for others is done. Rosters are posted on Saturday of work parties and their duties for the next day. These rosters are arranged by the departmental heads at their business meeting on the Friday evening of each week. The vil-

lages around are surveyed and lists of poor and needy
families are made and those without farm implements and
animals, and of widows and orphans. A party is then al-
lotted to the particular task, and that party takes the implements and animals needed. Lists are also made of roads,
bridges and other public utilities in the district in need of

repair.

In chapter one I mentioned a bog we came through on the day I arrived. One day I asked if anything had been done for this quagmire to the north of the village. "Come and see," said Mr. Ching.

Beyond living memory that bog had troubled the district. When we arrived, the finishing touches were being put to a solid stone structure, the show bridge of the district. The quagmire would trouble it no longer.

At this point my diary says, "The Communists are now coming to learn from the Christians, and their former arrogance has largely vanished."

The way in which these people keep Sunday has produced a very notable victory. Instead of being another cause for persecution it has become a day of praise and joy and unity.

EDUCATION

It has become necessary to change their classroom methods of teaching. Everybody in the Homes of Jesus is of course literate, but Christian schools became illegal as soon as the Communists took over control. The Chia-ting were allowed to carry on their schools. How and why is this?

The children all went out to work in the fields in the early morning. Many a time have Heng-shin and I watched them at work, weeding or picking grubs (insect pests are bad in China), or gleaning, and always with a diligence and joy that was remarkable. Since there were no games to call them away, they made a game of their work. Competitions and hurrying hither and thither were their playtime. Only once did I see quarrelling or bullying. There may have been more but I did not see it, and I had plenty of opportunity for observation. I was therefore interested to see how this case would be dealt with. It was the same boy I noticed several times, and apparently so did others also, for the next time I saw him he was suspended from school and at work in the carpenter's shop under the control of older men.

Suddenly in the midst of the children's activities the teacher appeared. All then gathered in the shade of a tree, and school began in earnest. If necessary a blackboard and textbooks were brought, all of which were made by the teachers themselves.

On wet days they carded and spun wool and thread, or husked maize (I am speaking of what I have seen). Spinning wool seems particularly the work of the boys, while the girls spin cotton thread for weaving into cloth. The teachers supervised during these sessions, and without interrupting their activities any subject on the curriculum could be dealt with by them. All that a visitor would see was a room full of children doing manual work.

They had a school magazine, written and illustrated by themselves. It was quite up to the standard of our school magazines at home.

Individuals about the compound showed their abilities in various ways. As an example, Sheng-yen, the blacksmith's striker, was assistant choir conductor. I saw him conduct sections of Handel's *Messiah;* other former scholars showed by their aptitudes how deeply the work of the teachers had gone.

As I have already pointed out, the farm workers, the carpenters, the blacksmiths, the bookbinders all had their theme songs, each of which was being constantly modified and improved. Their zest left no room for inertia. On the blackboards one saw statements of the day's plans, often summed up by a jingle rhyme, and the best of these were kept. It was all a continuation of school; the schoolroom did not end their student days, nor their study of literary forms.

The tiny tots, conducted by Tsi-sheng, the wife of the blacksmith, went through their action songs just as children do at home. Sunday School was managed much as it is with us, but was more orderly.

The village children around also come in for their special times of instruction. Their standard was far behind that of the Chia-ting children, but they were not forgotten and were given special periods on Sundays and holidays. I was touched to see a dumb village girl standing with her village group on the chapel platform and making feeble attempts to copy their actions. How different would have been her lot in an ordinary heathen village only those who have seen heathen China know. Whence comes the spirit which has produced our schools and asylums for the deaf, dumb, and blind? Think not that any heathen country has these, nor is there any place of refuge for the insane.

FAMILY LIFE

The Communists need armies; bigger and better armies is the constant demand. Odd as it may seem, there is a man-power shortage in China. War has been an endemic evil for the past forty years. The regime of Chiang-kai-shek is not to be judged too harshly. It proved its worth in this, that during the time in which it held undisputed sway there was relative peace and good government. That was before the Japanese attack in 1936.

But there is a shortage of men, as witness the number of unmarried girls in North China before the Communist dealt with the situation in their own way. Dr. Bessie and Helen Tso told me this, thus verifying my own observations.

It was obvious that in the farms around labour was at a premium, and frequently there was no labour to be had. Whole families, including little girls and very old men, were a common sight in the fields.

But now every girl must be married. Cannon-fodder is needed, and the Chinese have a very similar idiom to ours. Some squads of soldiers are composed of half male and half female, always in pairs, and not necessarily married. The male is "responsible" for the girl soldier. It is no un-common sight to see an overloaded girl soldier fall from fatigue or to suckle her baby by the roadside.

All in the Party are of course expected to be married, and the children are put into crêches. They told us that among normal children in these crêches the mortality is more than 30 per cent. In open-eyed admiration at the kindergartens of the Chia-ting the Communists asked, "How do you make the nurses love the children?"

Local officials have the power to force any girl to be married, and thus any girl over fifteen is in danger. This is the situation. How have the Christians met it?

In Chia-ting communities every young woman was either engaged or married to a Christian. There is among them no thought of marriage with a non-Christian; no such thing as a mixed marriage. I watched as closely as possible the way in which young people were guided and brought together. It was a privilege I had of being present with the elders in council when engagements were contracted.

Very soon after an engagement the marriage took place in an extremely impressive ceremony. This was followed by a wedding breakfast and honeymoon. All of this was a complete break with the old heathen form; even the word "honeymoon" is exactly translated from English and has come to be in common use.

Expectant mothers are given very efficient prenatal care. Mothers who have duties in the large central Homes put their children into the kindergarten and attend them under guidance until they are weaned. Then the parents may be sent out into village churches where they have homes of their own, or their home may become the nucleus of the village church, if there was no previous one.

Conditions and situations vary. Some parents live permanently in the central or mother Home. Their children are kept in the nursery and kindergarten; later they go to school, and then to one of the departments to learn a trade. While the children are young the parents see them at regular intervals. The children are always well and tastefully dressed, in marked contrast to the adults, who dress very poorly in patched, often purposely patched, garments, which are always spotlessly clean. As I stated earlier, when I first saw MaChuang village, I was amazed at the beauty of the children's dresses. The mothers and nurses no doubt find this an outlet for their taste and artistry. What an answer this is to Communist squalor! And no objection can be made to it, for the needs of the rising generation are overstressed by the Communists.

For adults fine clothes are taboo, and a danger to the one who dresses in them. A grown-up seeks, no matter what his financial status or position, to look poverty-stricken. It seems, however, that the position is changing, as it has changed in Russia. I heard many unguarded remarks outside MaChuang about "having the old landlord under a new name; he's now called a Communist."

The ordinary people are usually patched and filthy. One can travel through scores of villages with dirty, unkempt inhabitants and children, and houses we would not bed an animal in. The surprise with which Communists first saw Ma-Chuang with its scores of healthy people in clean garments, was very marked. But the children struck them with nothing else but awe, and they gazed at them in unstinted admiration. Any new group of Communists always asked to see the children first, and like the Queen of Sheba, they marvelled at very much the same things—their housing, their knowledge, and the wisdom of their nurses and attendants, the food of their tables, their manners and grace before meals, and above all, their dress.

These things come only from Christ. "I am come that they might have life, and that they might have it more abundantly" (John 10: 10).

Welfare Work

Let me refer particularly to three branches of their work, which have surpassed even the theories of the Communists: communal farming, medical work, and trade.

Here are quotations from letters I received in 1951. Dr. Bessie Chen wrote:

"I will let Helen write about our conference, which was quite a success and different this year. I talked on Midwifery; Doctors Feng and Chu talked on Medicine and Public Health. Others again talked on bee-keeping, others on sugar-making from beet and from barley. From visitors and brethren of other Homes and Christian communities we had talks on their living conditions and health.

"Representatives from the Communist authorities in

Taian attended our conference and received much benefit. One of them gave us talks on present-day politics. We all listened quietly and carefully. [I smiled when I read this.] When they left they showed their satisfaction for all they had seen and heard."

"Two teachers from this Home, a man and a woman, have been asked to start a night school for beginners in a neighbouring village. Day classes for the women in the same village have also been organized by the Communists, and they have put us in control." [Even the enthusiasm which these Christians brought to this work was insufficient, and eventually the classes stopped of themselves; the heathen scholars ceased to attend.]

"A commercial society has been organized by us and the Ching-chia-hang Home of Jesus to facilitate the buying and selling of all sorts of things, for the public as well as for ourselves. Heng-shin has been busy all day in this matter. The Communist authorities were very much surprised and inspired to see us so earnest and sincere in rendering this service to the public. A small piece of land has been loaned to us by the Communists at Taian railway station, and we will open a restaurant there for poor people."

This, I take it, is the "light" and "salt" of Christianity in operation. These Chinese Christians know this and have said as much. It is neither cleverness nor daring that the Easterner needs, but a moral background. A Chinese will learn to drive and understand a car in a few weeks, but it will be in its maintainance that he will break down. It is for this reason that a Hindu can graduate with high honours in medicine, but if he is not employed by the government, he will presently sink gradually to the level of his village forbears. It is not education that the East needs, but something deeper. Out of this deeper thing, the desire to be educated will arise spontaneously. Their need is Life. A true Christian will never remain uneducated. The first thing a Chinese countryman does after he has been converted is to learn to read. Mr. Ching constantly mentioned apathetic old country women, who had been practically slaves all their lives, transformed

overnight. " Transformed by the renewing of your mind,"
is the way St. Paul puts it. " It is from such that we get our
best and keenest theologians," Mr. Ching says.

The first Earl of Birkenhead said something to the effect
that St. Paul's mind was the greatest mind of all time. What
is the power that can take an old Chinese peasant woman
and almost overnight give her a mind that can comprehend
St. Paul?

AGRICULTURE

After I had left MaChuang, while I was standing in a group
of Chinese, I asked, " What is the average holding of each
adult in this district?"

The answer was, " One-third of an acre."

" How much then," I asked, " is sufficient for one man's
food?"

" From half an acre one person can get sufficient food to
live."

" The inference is therefore," I said, " that nearly the
whole rural population is living at starvation point."

" That is so," was the answer.

The Communists pride themselves on their system of land
tenure. I should rather say theory, for as yet their system
has to be proved. Every soul in Shantung will in the end
have an acre of land, they say. Force may be necessary!

In MaChuang the amount of land tilled is forty-three
acres in all, and there are nearly five hundred souls living in
this Christian community. This means that there is less than
one-tenth acre per person. There are two other large Homes
within twenty miles on either side. Only the greatest
efficiency can enable each to live adequately. What can the
Communists say in the face of this demonstration?

But there is something else involved. Formerly the land
owned by the Chia-ting was in numerous small pieces, scattered in various places over the countryside. These pieces
have been exchanged and manipulated until they are now
all concentrated around the Home buildings. In general it
may be said that it has become possible for farming

machinery to be used. To concentrate holdings in China is something beyond the power of human nature to accomplish. Land has been divided and subdivided between fathers and sons down the centuries. This is the great reason, which is ignored by theorizing, statistical economists, why farming is restricted to the use of hoe and reaping hook. The economist's theories in general are wrong. The heathen farmer still uses his reaping hook, not because he is mentally backward but because of his moral backwardness.

How can one of these farmers use a tractor on a piece of land no bigger than a backyard? If farming is to be modernized and machinery used, as Communism dictates, then these tiny holdings must be converted into larger ones, or the use of machinery is impossible. The Christians are accomplishing this miracle by forbearance and love. Can the Communists do it? They say they are going to, and they may possibly succeed by force.

The agrarian problem was not nearly so great in Russia as in China. Perhaps nothing but war and bloodshed on a still greater scale lie before China. One trembles to think of what is involved, not only for China, but also for the world. God has raised up a witness in China that Communist theories can be put into practice, not by Communists, but by those whom they despise. Man is so constituted that coercion spells his ruin, but only by coercion can Communist theories be put into practice. How wonderful to see these theories, and better than these, being practised by love!

I must, however deal in detail with this difficulty of concentrating many small holdings of land into one large piece. Tractors and machinery cannot be used on tiny parcels of land. The Ye-Su Chia-ting therefore, as I have already mentioned, set about collecting its holdings into one large farm. Nothing would convince one of the intractability of human nature more than a study of the Chia-ting's dealings with its neighbours over the last twenty years. Here is a case in point:

There is a most delectable corner of land right in the midst of the Chia-ting holdings. The owner of this piece cannot use it himself, neither can the Chia-ting, and it deforms part of their beautiful compound. The owner knows that his cupidity has damaged him irrevocably, yet every time terms are settled a night's reflection reveals to him the possibility of further gains. Every new concession from the Christians has brought a new demand from him. The first arrangement was a piece of land similar in size, near his own village He then demanded a well in addition. This was granted, and a well was dug for him. Then he demanded machinery and pump for the well. Then he wanted a horse-works to work the pump. His next move was for an animal to work it. Then he wanted trees to be planted near the well, and they had to be big ones (the Chinese are very clever at transplanting quite large trees). Finally, he wanted additional money. At this point the negotiations had stuck, when I left.

I do not think for one moment that such indecision and cupidity were a studied policy. The poor man was being driven by his own "vile" nature; he was being driven as with a goad, and could not help himself even if he would.

In many cases during these protracted negotiations I have seen the direct hand of God, by sudden poverty and death, bringing negotiations to a climax and forcing the hands of heathen negotiators. But in most cases, temperance and love won the day. This is how we learn forbearance and tolerance, say the Christians. Uncontrolled, tigerish human nature can only be dealt with by "purges," say the Communists.

Again, the hedge of trees in many places abuts on a neighbour's land. Unreasonable ones have, on the plea that the roots are absorbing nourishment from their land, deeply trenched and cut the roots of the trees, deforming them in places.

Mr. Ching, far from being offended, glories in these difficulties because of the many triumphs of grace seen in intransigent neighbours being won over and converted.

"On the other hand," he says, "how can I have my own corners rubbed off and straightened, if others don't rub and twist me?" "Uncut, unwrought gems are valueless," says the Chinese aphorism.

A more serious difficulty, unknown to us, is the extra-ordinary one of stealing land. What land hunger there is in China! An unwatched neighbour will gradually dig away the land bordering on his field, and transport it to enlarge his own land. The road outside one of the Chia-ting gates was thus stolen, leaving an impassable hole. The thief anticipated that the Christians would have to fill it up with soil of their own. The digging was all done at night and secretly.

An unwanted grave mound is moved in a very simple way from my land to yours. If a man buys another man's field with graves in it, then the graves are inviolate. But nibbling at one side and building up the other will shift the most in-convenient grave to a more convenient spot. It takes time, of course.

Heng-shin said to me one day, " I wonder how many graves in China have bones in them? If they are isolated, then they are almost certain to be nothing but a mound of earth."

Chapter Four

Incidents from the life of the Ye-Su Chia-ting

I HEARD THIS TESTIMONY FROM THE CHAPEL PLATFORM IN MaChuang. The wife of the leader involved was speaking. She said:

" The leader of our church, my husband, was to have a village trial for harbouring Nationalist soldiers. He was already in gaol. These trials invariably end in a horrible death. He was to be buried alive, and he was not guilty, for the soldiers were fleeing and had forced us to allow them to sleep in the chapel. All was ready, the stage set, and the judge and accusers had arrived.

" The day before the trial, several of us were together in the chapel praying for my husband, when a chicken came in and laid an egg. It made such a noise that it disturbed our prayers, so I got up and caught it and, little thinking of the result of my action, tied a note and some money to the chicken's leg to pay for the egg. An hour or so later, the landlady of the village inn came down the street followed by a gentleman. A crowd was following. The landlady simply said, ' These are the Christians,' and withdrew.

" The gentleman said he was the Communist judge and asked, ' Did you write this note?'

" I said, ' Yes,' for it was the note I had tied to the hen's leg.

" ' Did you tie this ten cents to the hen's leg?'

" Again I said, ' Yes.'

" ' That hen belonged to the landlady of the inn where I am staying.' He then asked us of our beliefs, and the reason for this uncommon and exceptional act. With great simplicity he said, ' Such honesty I have not seen before. How did you become like this?' We told him of Jesus. The upshot was that there was no trial the next day; it was quashed by the moved and amazed judge."

While I was working in the hospital, Christians were being "registered" by the Communists. An old countryman was called. He had been well coached beforehand by his pastor, as had others; they were Presbyterians. When it came to the point he refused all advice and said he would reply to the Communist's questioning as the Lord gave him utterance at that moment.

"What has Christianity done for you?" asked the Communist official.

"Made me a better man," replied the old farmer.

"Is this so?" he asked the assembled villagers. This was a public trial.

There was a very emphatic, "Yes," from those assembled. It was reported that his farm used to be the dirtiest and worst in their village and now it was the best.

"How did this happen?"

"I was a drunkard and an opium smoker, nothing could rid me of those two vices, and my farm had been brought to ruin. But I accepted Jesus as my Saviour, and He changed me. He enabled me to break with both opium and drink. My fellow villagers can now testify to these things and my farm is now the best. Ask them." This is the sort of reply with which the Communists cannot deal.

Here is another testimony told in the chapel at MaChuang, while I was present :

"I had a dream and told it to my husband when I woke. In my dream I was in a village about forty li* away, I saw a man and his wife preparing breakfast. All they had in the big pot was grass and leaves.

"I said to my husband : 'Meo-meo village has turned to the Lord and started a Chia-ting. You must take them some grain.'

About 14½ miles.

" 'How do you know?' he asked. I told him my dream. He started out immediately with two sacks of grain on each side of his wheelbarrow, and some bean-curd to sell for incidental expenses. Money was not used along the road he took and so he bartered the bean-curd for rice bowls and chop-sticks. On arrival he found things just as I had dreamed. The Holy Spirit had fallen on the man and his wife, and they had given all they had to the poor. My husband gave them the grain for their breakfast, and bowls and chop-sticks as well. There was a feast of joy in which the neighbours joined; many immediately turned to the Lord, when they saw the grace that was given."

This is the power of the early church! What can stop it? And what a Chinese flavour it all has!

An influential member of the Ye-Su Chia-ting is Pastor Chow, and he is the only one I have heard addressed by his title. He is an ordained Presbyterian minister.

His wife's great sorrow was that she was childless. If any one doubts the story of Sarah's suggestion to Abraham then they need doubt no longer. The pastor had repeatedly rejected his wife's suggestion that he should take another wife. In this he differed from Abraham.

Pastor Chow remained deaf to his wife's suggestions. He is the leader of the young people's parties as they go out evangelizing, for his chief work has been building up bodies of isolated and distant believers. Up to the time when I left, his work was still being carried on, and possibly may still be, for these people have so amazed their Communist rulers that anything is possible.

When the pastor's work of preaching and teaching was finished, I frequently found him alone in the cotton field, tending the plants or picking the cotton. Possibly it was his time and place for meditation.

The Communists had their spies everywhere. I was told by a commissar as he took out a sheaf of papers referring to me, how many times I had been seen working in the fields. "It's all in your dossier," he said.

In these Homes there is always a bustle of many com-
ings and goings—conferences, study circles, choir practices,
new believers arriving and introducing themselves and being
attended to.   Classes including Bible study are continuous,
and all branches of technical work from horticulture to building are taught.   In the midst of all this activity is the constant sound of singing, for choir gatherings are frequent, and
spontaneous singing is heard everywhere.

I met many university graduates among them.   One day
quite a noted lawyer put down his buckets of dung for a
chat.   It sometimes seemed as though the more menial the
work, the higher was the spiritual status of the one who did
it :   " If any man desire to be first, the same shall be last of
all, and servant of all " (Mark 9 : 35).   This is not just one
more passage of Scripture with them, but something to be
obeyed, a command and a stimulus.

I watched with interest the departure of young married
couples to assist in the work in newly opened villages.   Only
newly married couples were sent.

It will be a long time before I forget the departure of

Chuin-hsiang and his wife to initiate work in Hankow. This was immediately after it had been captured by the Communists from the Nationalists. This young man was a Peking University Science graduate. He and his wife proposed to start the work in Hankow by peddling bean-curd from door to door. Their missionary equipment consisted of what they could carry in their hands.

As a student he was an atheist. After his graduation he went home for a holiday. His home was in Shantung, not far from MaChuang, the headquarters of the Chia-ting. He arrived home and found all his relatives ashamed and horror-struck because his sister was, as they said, demon-possessed. He scouted the idea, fortified as he was with the assurance of his Western learning. Scornful of the ignorance of his relatives, he went in to see his sister. She was sitting in a daze and he could scarcely recognize her. His pretty, vivacious sister of a year ago now looked like a senseless old crone. Suddenly to his astonishment and fear a man's voice spoke with her lips, while her face was agonized and convulsed. They called in necromancers, but their incantations were powerless. The voice taunted them, saying that the only one he feared was Jesus. The pastor and some other Christians came. They prayed, and then in the Name of Jesus commanded the demon to come out of her. The man's voice replied, " I'll go," and then again, " I'll go," but fainter; then a series, " I'll go, I'll go, I'll. . ." until the voice was lost in the distance.

When Chuin-hsiang told me the story, he added, " My sister was well from that hour, and I became a Christian from that hour."

On my arrival in MaChuang I was given a young man as a valet by the name of Ching-ts'ong. His wife had been brought up in a Christian family; she was a dear girl named Leah, and a very clever nurse. She nearly always came out top in the examinations held among the nursing staff. These were really tests held by the nursing staff among themselves and supervised by those in charge.

These two, Ching-ts'ong and his wife, gave me the most faithful service all the time I was with them. He did the most menial jobs for me, jobs which I never asked of him. When I thanked him he told me straight out that being thanked rather dulled the keen edge of his service for the Lord. I gradually learned that this was not simply a gesture, but a real attitude deeply seated in his spiritual life. Such a revolution in one's foreign way of thinking is not easily come by. But it indicates what a missionary to the " heathen " has to contend with. In spite of myself, I did as he suggested, and thanked God instead for his faithful service.

He told me that his work was his only method of preaching, and so he was surprised that I had pressed the matter of the thanks. Just after my arrival, since he had been allocated to me, I called him. He " waited not upon the order " of his coming, but came running at once. I wondered to myself, if after a few months, he would run like that. He served me all the two years I was there, and to the last day he never changed. I cannot but testify to this and glorify God for His grace in that young man.

Another young fellow, named Hu-chao, whose responsibility was the fowls and rabbits, was on his way to the university when the Lord called him—he had just matriculated. His chicken coops were sanded and limed every day; with glass in their roofs they were well-aired and lighted. They had been built by him and an older man, and were a constant source of comment by the Communists. Love of his charges entered into his work, for one day I caught him silently weeping over some of his rabbits which had died.

Another of those whose work testified for them was an older brother named Ru-shun. He had had a mechanical training, but live things interested him more. He it was who put the hens' eggs in the rooks' nests. Three weeks later he climbed the elms and brought down the fluffy yellow chicks. We all laughed at the shock these little changelings must have caused their black foster-parents.

Beside these living incubators, he had others which he had

built himself. From these he brought out hundreds of chickens, geese and ducks in a year. His were also the pigeon lofts, from which I had many a tasty meal. His fancy pigeons interested me immensely—most of them were unknown to me—pouters, fantails, and others of which I knew only the Chinese name.

The Forestry Department had as its head a graduate of

Nanking University. He seemed to know all about tree culture and was a most interesting conversationalist. Transplanting, pruning, grafting and tree surgery were his speciali-
ties. They could transplant trees large enough to need twenty
or thirty men to carry them. I saw a whole row of large
trees that had been transplanted in this way. In one spot
the transplanted tree died three times. They dug out and
changed all the soil before they finally got a tree to grow
there. No wonder their orchards on Tai-shan were such a
picture, and that by them the whole of Tai-shan was being
transformed. These Christians were transplanting about
20,000 trees a year on this bare mountain. The seedlings were
taken from their own nurseries in the late winter and transported about thirty miles.

All these activities were harmonized and controlled by the
Friday evening leaders' meeting. (Anyone was free to attend
although it was held especially for leaders' discussions.)
Here all their policy was formulated. I was an honorary
member and usually attended these interesting and instructive meetings.

Quite apart from these routine matters, which may seem so
exceptional to us, extraordinary incidents like the following
happened from time to time.

A section of road and a dike outside their district needed
repairing. The Communist call of conscripted labour included
young men both from the Chia-ting and also those from a nearby heathen village. This village had shown continuous enmity
to the Gospel and had in many ways proved a great trial to
MaChuang. They had proved themselves intractible to every
advance and now they were proving themselves implacable
enemies.

This particular call-up was an excellent chance for impos-
ing on and harming the Christians, for the heathen village
elder was in charge of the operations. Half the work was to
be done by each village, but this elder said the Communist
order was that MaChuang was to send men to both sections.
He sent his people only to repair the dike. As the burden on
the Christians increased, so did that on the heathen corres-

pondingly decrease; so much so, that in time all the work was being done by the former. There was a time limit for the completion of the work, and this particular Friday evening meeting marked the halfway stage. Hen-shin rose and reported the unfairness of the situation. What was to be done? Should they report to the Communist authorities. This was vetoed and their justification placed in God's hands. God would work for them; if not, they were well content. I was reminded of Daniel's friends, " Our God is able to deliver us . . . but if not . . ."

On the Monday Communist overseers unexpectedly arrived. The elder did all in his power to keep the visit confined to the dike, where his men were doing part of the work. But the Communists also visited the road and asked why the Ma-Chuang Christians were at work in both places. Heng-shin told him that such were his orders. " Orders from whom?" " From this village elder," said Heng-shin.

The elder was caught and Heng-shin had to plead to keep him from gaol. The only punishment he received was that his people had to complete both places, but there was a further development. The elder got himself into yet more trouble. On the following Friday night I heard the end of the matter. He was now in danger of his life for accepting bribes. (This was a very sore point just at this time with the Communists. They had promised there would be no more corruption in their government, in contrast to the Nationalists.) The elder had twisted the road in one place to avoid an ancestral grove; in another, so as not to cut off the corner of a man's field, and had been bribed to do this.

Heng-shin was now placed in charge as the only one who was trustworthy. All the Christians were sent home, and the Ye-Su Chia-ting placed over the village. The Christians' yoke was easy, although they were given by the Communists complete control of the heathen.

I have noticed in these Friday night meetings a spirit of contrition and confession. If faults are to be confessed, it is here in the presence of one another that it is done. I could write much on Communist " brain washing " and confession meetings, which are a peculiar phenomenon and sinister, in that they are a counterfeit of Christian confession " to one another." It would do us good to meditate on this. Satan's system copies God's very closely. Communists confess from the fear of one another; Christians confess from the fear and love of God.

At the beginning of 1949, I had a particularly acute and agonizing attack of peripheral neuritis. During four painful weeks, Miss Helen Tso was my nurse, with Ching-ts'ong as assistant.

During this time I saw what utter surrender of self is, and what nursing can be when it is done as a vocation. There can be no doubt that the nursing staff is the centre and heart of the modern hospital. Florence Nightingale's supreme sense of a nurse's vocation has been caught by these Chinese. Helen Tso had the responsibility of night duty, and while doing this carried on all her day duties as well. On my sick bed I wondered how it was possible, yet there she was with the same quiet serenity, when the need arose.

This was a period of great anxiety, and to meet the need whole days were set apart for fasting and prayer. Miss Tso fasted like Esther, tasting neither food nor water for three days and three nights. I have heard a Chinese preacher say that there are circumstances in which Heaven will be moved for us only if we are first moved on our own behalf. If we are to possess the power which the early church exercised, then apparently we must pay the same price.

One day Mr. Ching said to me. " It is not power that we need, but a deeper death. Oh, that the purpose of Calvary might be seen in me!"

The bethren then thought well to send me, after obtaining a Communist pass, to the Union Hospital in Tsinan, about three days to the north. Dr. Smyllie was still there, although the city had been " liberated " for some time by the Communists. Under his able ministrations I gradually improved, and the time came for me to return to MaChuang. Travel was rigorously controlled, and the young commissar, whom I interviewed, sent two soldiers to "protect" me. He told me that Communism would sweep Christianity away overnight. "Christianity is thistledown. It is not one of our worries."

He asked me about the church at MaChuang, and I asked him why he did not come and see for himself. After a pause he said, "I will." Next morning, sure enough, he was at the station. As we travelled South, he told me what Communism was going to do in the world. "In England, America, Australia—nothing will stop us."

We arrived in MaChuang, and he was shown to his room. I went to mine. I did not see him again for three days, and then he came to say good-bye. A change in his attitude was immediately apparent. He appeared to be humbled and chastened. "I have seen," he said, "something which I did not know existed in the world. This is what we Communists want to do; we won't do it in a hundred years!" We shook hands and parted.

And so the Homes of Jesus are thus witnessing to the Communists. There is no doubt that these dear folk have peculiarities. Dr. Samuel Johnson said to Boswell that "uncommon parts require uncommon opportunities for their exertion." At MaChuang we find both the uncommon parts and the uncommon opportunities, and how could they have carried on in these tragic and awful circumstances, if they did not have them?

Many have found fault with them because of certain peculiarities. What has been called their excess of emotion has displeased some. Sometimes I found it hard to bear. Once I calmed myself by wondering what I would have thought if I had seen Jacob lift up his voice and weep when he saw Rachel for the first time (Gen. 29: 11). It was not long in my case before all their peculiarities were hidden and swept away by a vision of their overwhelming love of the Lord Jesus and their allegiance to Him to the death.

I sat with enthusiastic young Chinese in a new church vestry and heard their stories. This church was a landmark in the greyish drab Chinese village, for it was of red brick. Something had gone wrong in the kiln, and the young people found that their bricks had turned out red instead of the usual slate grey. It was the first case of red brick in that district, and so the series of kilns had continued to the end until the church was completed.

There was revival in the district and parties were coming in to recount their experiences. All was well except in one place called Meo village. The young people from this village were mystified. Prayer had been made, exhortation given, idols had been taken down and burned, many in the village had been apparently converted, yet all remained as before; there was no revival and no manifestation of the work of the Holy Spirit.

The village elders looked at one another. They knew what was wrong and they also knew now that our God is a God of knowledge, by whom actions are weighed. There was hidden sin and Jehovah saw it. He clearly was not like their idols. The 139th Psalm became real to them: " Yea the darkness hideth not from Thee but the night shineth as the day, the darkness and the light are both alike to Thee."

" Come," said the elders, " and we will show you what is wrong." Picks and shovels were produced, and their earth gods were dug up in pots from back yards, in which they were buried. When the last had been removed, destroyed and burned, revival began. So the rejoicing in that village mingled with awe and the fear of God.

I learned that the custom of burying the earth gods was peculiar to this village and not known in any of the others.

A Chinese Christian came with me to a market place and we watched a countryman at a butcher's stall. The butcher was giving him bits from every part of the pig and he was threading them on a string, an eye, piece of the ear, entrails; all were included. " Let's question him," said my companion in answer to my query as to what he was doing. " He has sworn to give a pig to his idol if it would grant his request; apparently his prayer has been granted and this is the result ".

" But has your idol no eyes, can it not see you are deceiving it?" said I.

" But the idol also deceives me; why should I not deceive it?" was the countryman's reply.

About this time we crossed the hills to one of the villages revival had visited. There was much coming and going and joy was on every side. Singing and voices raised in prayer were very marked. We sat in the chief guest room with the village headman and asked how it happened.

" It is quite a long story," he said, " and began over two years ago, when my second son, Old-two, bought a Bible on the market place. We knew it was a foreign book and we warned him not to read it. But apparently he did and we noticed a great change coming over him. I taxed him with reading the book in secret; he admitted it and said that he had given his heart to the Saviour Jesus, whose story was given in it.

" His elder brother, Old-big, and I determined to put a stop to his involvment with this foreign religion, so we burned the book and treated him so badly that he became sick and died. We thought that that was the end of it. But about two weeks ago Old-big came in tired from the harvest field and went to sleep without having his meal. In spite of all our efforts he did not wake until the third day, then he suddenly sat up, called us all and said he had seen Old-two.

" Gradually the whole village gathered as he told his dream; although he would not admit that it was a dream, it was too real he said."

Then began a marvellous story from the old headman to which we listened enthralled. Old-big in his dream had seen what St. John describes in Revelation chapters 21 and 22; the River, the Tree of Life, the Fruit, the Book of Life, the Golden Streets—all were there, and Old-big had never read the Bible. Old-big had suddenly found himself transported to this place and there was Old-two coming to meet him with his arms outstretched in welcome and a smile of joy upon his face, with no resentment, no remembrance of the wrong that had been done him. " He thought that I too had died, but had first received Jesus," broke in Old-big. Two men in white then took us to the centre of the city where we saw a large book, in which the names of all the saved were written. Old-two showed me his name. We looked for mine, but it was not there, neither was Father's name nor Mother's nor the name of anyone from this village."

" What a cry of anguish and lamentation went up from us all," said the old man. " We fell on our faces and cried to God."

" All this took place not much more than a week ago. We sent for someone to help us, and found that revival had broken out in other villages also, and there were you brothers and sisters of the Ye-su Chia-ting, for you had come into the district."

This book would be the poorer if I did not add something about a Russian lady who was saved from a life of degradation by the Ye-Su Chia-ting. Born in Southern Siberia, she met and married a Chinese landowner, and lived with him on the Russian-Manchurian border. A few happy prosperous years passed and three sons were born. Then in the early 30's, the Japanese invasion burst upon them. They lost all, and her husband was killed. Before he died he gave her his home address in Shantung. Having no other resources, she set out for her husband's home village, thinking that it would be something like her happy Manchurian home. She was shocked to find her father-in-law an opium smoker, living in a squalid Chinese village in such squalor as she had not seen before. All the family patrimony was being spent on opium, and the father-in-law was incensed at having four more mouths to feed. Mrs. Chang, for that was her name, could speak no Chinese, but she soon sensed that plans were afoot to sell her to a brothel. By this time she had been reduced to rags and starvation, most of the little she had left being used to keep her three children alive.

It was at this point that the Ye-Su Chia-ting heard of her.

A Russian woman, report said, was in Meo village, about forty miles away. She was in rags, starving, and about to be sold into a brothel. No time was to be lost. Perhaps even then they were too late. Three of the brethren set out immediately with a barrow as a conveyance to try to persuade her and her three boys to go with them to MaChuang. When they arrived they found her like a tigress, unable to speak Chinese and fearing everybody. The three brethren were in a quandary, for she resisted all their approaches. In their utter perplexity, they knelt beside their barrow in prayer. That did it! When she saw them praying, memories of her girlhood immediately flooded back, the church in Russia she had attended, and the way in which the congregation and her parents used to kneel in prayer. The brethren's quest was successful; she gave in straightway and went with them.

She has been converted and is now an honoured member of the MaChuang Home of Jesus. Two of her sons are married to two sweet Chinese girls. Her third son has joined the Communists and she has lost sight of him. This is one of the few tragedies I experienced. All the family but this son live together and work for the Lord in MaChuang.

Chapter Five

Medical Work in MaChuang

A S I MENTIONED EARLIER, IT WAS THE INVITATION OF THE
Ye-Su Chia-ting to go and see the wounded that had been
left with them after the fighting that first brought me to
MaChuang.

The first case I saw was a Communist soldier, who had had
his foot shattered some time before. It had been amputated by
a Communist army doctor. The bone was sticking through,
covered only by a pinch skin-graft placed directly on the
granulating bone. Such a thing should never have been done.
A stump so formed is so tender that it cannot be used. We
would call it malpractice. I had to reoperate to give him a
usable stump. This was one of the cases which was blind-
folded in order that my presence might not be known to the
Communists.

Later the soldier said he knew all the time that a foreigner
was operating on him. We wondered why he had not reported to his authorities. The reason was that he had given
his heart to Christ. Later he applied for a pension. The
officer who was sent to interview him reviled him for " eating " a foreign religion. He answered, much to our surprise,
" But isn't what you have eaten a foreign religion, belonging
to Marx and Lenin?" Apparently nonplussed by his reply,
all the officer said was, " You can't beat these Christians in
argument."

The surgeon who had performed the operation was entirely
without principle, although quite up to standard in his technique. Western medicine will never last among the Communists, for the sufficient reason that it needs to rest on a
firmer basis than simple technique.

Dr. Bessie Chen was taken by the Communists and was

held by them for over a year. Her chief duty was to teach the ward attendants to operate on hernia.

Let me explain that simply to diagnose a hernia, apart altogether from the operation, is a difficult matter, fraught with all sorts of pitfalls even to an experienced surgeon. For an untrained man to attempt it spells disaster, and such Dr. Bessie found to be the case. The wounds of many of the cases were still unhealed after a year. She struggled month after month to get away, and only succeeded when she stated that she was suffering from appendicitis. She wanted me to operate on her.

The wards in the Communist hospital, Dr. Bessie said, were so dirty that she herself took a broom to sweep them. The superintendent came in at that moment and stopped her, saying that the servants would not respect her, if they saw her sweeping. " Quite simply I said to him, ' But I thought we were all equal!' " Dr. Bessie told me.

During the summer of 1949 a measles epidemic raged throughout the MaChuang area, and the mortality so the Communists said, was up to 80 per cent.

Our children were involved through a Communist child inadvertently admitted to the clinic. Sixty-three of our little ones took measles. Two died, one with the dreaded broncho-pneumonia. A mortality of 3 per cent was astounding news to the Reds. So impressed were they that they held a meeting in the chapel, and several hundred of them came with pencil and paper to find out how it was done. The chairman was a Communist. The questions asked were most revealing, for example, " How do you make the nurses take an interest in their work and love the children?", " How do you stop the nurses from stealing the drugs?" To questions like these practically the same answer was given, " If they have the Lord Jesus in their hearts, then all these questions are solved."

There were medical questions also but it was easy to see that the chairman had sensed something deeper. At the end of the meeting, which lasted about three hours, he summed up by saying, " Comrades, I see that unless we believe this religious superstition, we will not be able to manage a children's crêche."

We felt that the Communists, or some of them, were making shipwreck on a totally unsuspected rock. Morality, integrity and God they had ignored or denied, and they were being destroyed. This is a true interpretation of the passage, "Evil shall slay the wicked." How pointed and exact the Bible is! Such things are recognised, when experience has proved that it is so, and it is then too late to change.

How many young people are travelling this irrevocable road! If what I saw and heard in Shantung is any criterion, Communist public services are breaking down, not because there is any lack of brains, but simply for lack of integrity. Ruthless dictatorship seems to hold things together for a time, but the descent to the pit is sure, even if slow as measured by our life span. Eventually savagery supervenes. Science has yet to prove that savage races were not at one time more cultured than they are now and have "devolved."

Communist soldiers and officers, who visited Ma-Chuang clinic while I was there, were different from the rank and file of Chinese patients. So many of their troubles took on a nervous trend. One could see there was strain in their lives. This was admitted by many to whom I put the question directly. Hatred and malice are prime causes of digestive upsets. Physiologists are emphasizing this in their search for the causes of peptic ulcer of the stomach and duodenum. Twenty or thirty years ago the cause was sought in infection, the so-called "septic focus"; the search is now shifting to the emotions.

This was our experience in Ma-Chuang. These Communist patients were mostly living lives of fear and hatred due to the constant spying on one another. Among them there was a very high percentage of symptoms of gastric and duodenal ulcer. I saw and operated on many cases of ruptured acute ulcer, a dangerous procedure which was later abandoned. At any time a death might be laid at our door by these unstable people, not only unstable but ultra-suspicious. Doing medical work among them is a dangerous occupation.

Suicide was terribly common, and little was thought of it. They quite openly admitted how hopeless and meaningless life was to them. What they called "brain washing" had mystified and confused them, and changed all life's values. What a devilish thing is being done to the young life of China! It is so difficult to get at the back of it all. A private conversation leaves one confused, groping and uncomprehending, and further interviews only make the gloom deeper. There is a true Light that "lighteth every man that cometh into the world." One cannot help feeling that this is what is at stake.

All the terms we use they use also, but with a different value and interpretation. But this is not all; the perversion and subversion go much deeper. They value truth, or say they do, but it is impossible to tell them the truth. Some Russians asked a friend of mine how many Republicans Truman killed, when he became President. Surprised, my friend answered, "None."

"What's the use of further talk?" said the Russians. "This man can't tell the truth."

What an awful nemesis it is that makes a mind believe a lie! The gold of words is extracted, and base metal put into circulation as gold. It seems that they are treating modern science, including medicine, in the same way. I operated on a case, who told me his appendix had been removed, but the appendix was still there, and I am convinced that nothing had been done but the skin incision. Another case had a large scar, and in it a very painful hernia. On operating, I found the bowel in among the abdominal muscles. No apparent effort had been made to restore the tissues to their normal relationships.

Chiang-kai-shek's government may have been corrupt, but it had made surprising progress in putting its medical services straight, and eliminating such malpractices as these. Communism seems to encourage them.

A cleaner in the operating theatre, after seeing one or two operations, became a "doctor" in the army on the strength of this. Looking for bullets he twice cut through the main artery of the thigh, and the victims bled to death.

Words are inadequate to describe the callousness and carelessness of the men who take this work upon them, and their outrageous confidence and colossal vanity. Peculiarly they trusted us, and Communist soldiers and officers flocked to us and submitted to the most serious surgical procedures at our hands.

A few successful cases at the beginning and I had their entire confidence. As always, an extreme in one direction soon has its resultant extreme in the other; their confidence and reverence became embarrassing.

We had of course to deal with the blind and did many cataracts. A blind old lady appeared, a cataract in each eye. The Communist doctor said that he had prepared the theatre for a demonstration. When I went in I found that a stage had been set up, occupied by what appeared to be a very partisan football crowd. There was to be a kind of village trial, and it was I who was to be tried! For the Communist said that he would do one eye and I would do the other. He had already told the crowd that he had had 90 per cent success with his cataract operations. He was obviously out to show me up. As was always the case in a Communist setting, the situation could become dangerous.

I could not withdraw and so I began the operation. I was nervous, and it was not long before I was in difficulties. The unfriendly anti-foreign onlookers sniggered and nudged one another. A little more of this and I would have panicked. But at this juncture I paused, dropped everything, prayed and regained my composure.

The operation then proceeded smoothly to a satisfactory conclusion; so satisfactory was it that the Communist was in a quandary. I could imagine what was passing in his mind; weighing up the chances, he decided not to take the risk.

" Please go on and do the other eye," he said.

There were Christians in the crowd and they told me how they had been praying for me. We had a great victory and the fickle Communist onlookers were now all on my side.

I was operating on a cancer of the lip in an old man. The operation was being done under local anaesthesia and there was much to be done; the patient was suffering some pain. Helen Tso took the old man's hand. "Remember," she said, "it is the Lord who suffers too. He bore our sickness and carried our infirmities." The old man was immediately silent, and bore all the rest of the operation without a murmur.

Mr. Ching preached about this old man that night, and the sermon touched the patient very closely for he was there on a stretcher. Mr. Ching said, "The further one travels on the way of life, and the nearer one approaches Him who is Life, the more one knows that miracles and outward manifestations are dangerous. Enter into the heart of our Lord's suffering. The way there is not the way of freedom from bodily infirmity and pain."

The local stationmaster brought his little girl, who had bone disease of the leg. An operation was necessary. I was surprised therefore, when he said he could not wait for the operation, but made immediate preparations to return to his work. This is not at all like a Chinese parent. "I cannot stay," he said, "we now have twenty-four-hour shifts, and I am doing the work that three men formerly did."

"Why don't you go on strike?" I said facetiously.

He changed colour, drew me aside and glancing over his shoulder said, "We dare not mention that word now."

The practice of midwifery is an ever-present source of care, thought, and work to a doctor in China. Both Dr. Bessie and Helen are most efficient obstetricians. I was only called in when the situation was beyond their strength. They constantly had hair-raising cases, for China's most degrading superstitions are concerned with childbirth. Is it possible to make it more agonizing than it is to the mother?

Just before I left MaChuang, Dr. Bessie came to me for advice. An old lady was accused by the whole countryside of being with child by a demon and she believed it herself.

How was she to convince her that it was not so? I said to her, " That should be easy, surely."

" Not so easy as you think. Helen and I have spent hours trying to convince her. We have already been to her home three times and are now going again."

This is a black picture, and but one superstition in many. Can legislation deal with this? It took Wesley's preaching to shift witchcraft out of Cornwall; that is an easily proved historic fact.

Two of our children died of measles during the great measles epidemic which struck North China. I was standing beside the cot of one of these little ones, while it was in *extremis*. We had done all we could. Mr. Ching came and stood beside me and began to pray for the child. " Now," I thought, " we will see a miracle." For Mr. Ching's early ministry had been born in miracle. But as he was praying the little one died.

When he heard that its breathing had ceased, he put his hand on my shoulder, and said, " Dear brother, three or four years ago that wouldn't have happened to me. If I had prayed for that child then, it would have lived. But things have changed since then, and I would not have it otherwise. Do you know that power can be a dangerous thing, even power from God? It can fill one with spiritual pride. It is not power that I choose but a deeper death. Oh, that the power of Calvary might be seen in me!"

That night he preached to about a thousand Christian Chinese on such Biblical characters as Balaam, Samson, and Saul, the king of Israel. " Were their lives in keeping with the power they had?"

Two Aspects of Medical Missionary Work

To be a Medical Missionary is not the easiest form of service on the mission field, and sometimes great determination is needed not only to win people's confidence but sometimes also to escape disaster.

To do a cataract operation in a Tibetan tent is not easy, but it has been done. So also goitres were removed in an adapted Tibetan hay loft, and eye operations were done on a flat roof. In this latter place we were shot at, while operating, as there was a blood feud on—so much for those who would have us believe in "the peace loving Buddhists of Tibet!" We found as we travelled that there was a blood feud on in nearly every encampment and village—thirty-two lives had already been lost in the one mentioned. We all, including the patient, tumbled down the notched tree-trunk, which served as a stairway.

Having accomplished this much, I thought that as there was an abdominal operation necessary in another village, we might do it without undue risk. The advantages were impressive; it meant an introduction into the village and an opportunity to preach and live the Gospel, for we would be there for several days.

I have used the phrase "live the Gospel"; that is if all went well. But what does one do, if things go wrong, and this operation did go wrong—the patient died suddenly under the anaesthetic. The village was at an altitude of over ten thousand feet and I used chloroform. The advantage of chloroform is that it is less bulky than ether or any other anaesthetic, but we reckoned without the altitude and paucity of oxygen supply. Under ordinary circumstances there is four times less margin of error than with ether, so we took all the precautions possible. I did not have a trained anaesthetist of course, so Edwin Carlson of the Christian and Missionary Alliance volunteered.

When I was last in the United States, Edwin, Carol his wife and I recapitulated that dreadful experience of more than twenty years ago in the fastnesses of Tibet. Like the broken soldier and the village preacher we,

"Wept o'er our wounds and tales of sorrow done—."

Edwin was the anaesthetist, my wife was my assistant at the operation. All went well, and I was preparing to finish, when Edwin gasped. "The patient has stopped breathing." All I could do was of no avail; the patient was dead. We were plunged into the situation we most dreaded, the worst we could have anticipated in our most pessimistic and fearful moments. There were many aspects to the danger we were in. We had broken several Tibetan superstitions, for the least of which only death could atone.

Now twenty years after I asked Edwin what had given him strength, so that for hours he held off that crowd of avenging Tibetans. It was not only me they wanted; they were intent on murdering us all, including little Bobbie of six summers, Carlson's son. The leaden hours passed, and eventually so did the danger. How we lived those hours again, and I could see the strain of it all still written on Edwin's face as we talked. Only in Heaven will we know what preaching the Gospel in heathen lands has cost in " blood, sweat and tears".

Praise God there is another side to this grim picture and so now I would like to mention some of the compensations : I want to point out how prayer changes things in a clinic.

Formerly, when I was in China, with extreme fatigue and distaste I would see clinics of over a hundred patients in a morning. How I longed to give up medical work. Fruitless toil it seemed to be, with all the valuable and lasting work left to the hospital evangelist and all the grind to me! I had neither the time nor inclination to see the good, if any, I was doing.

For about four years now in Hong Kong I have restricted the number of patients at a clinic to about fifty, never more. So now the work of dealing with spiritual problems is not left to the hospital evangelist. A revolution has taken place not only in the patient's attitude but also in mine; I no longer want to give up, discouragement is a thing of the past.

Let me go into further detail as to the way in which it works. Among the patients I saw one day was a country-man who lives in a village very near the Chinese border. When one prays with patients they will become interesting and lovable human beings, each with problems, which they do not hide, when they find the doctor looks upon them as something more than a test-tube with a chemical problem to solve.

I particularly noted this countryman because of the vivid

description he gave of his agony (he had peptic ulcer) and his certainty that death was only just round the corner. He had lost much weight, and life was a burden. Everything had been tried, including necromancers, witch-doctors and all the Government hospitals, he particularly mentioned the Queen Mary Hospital in which he had been an in-patient (this impressed me, because of the place the Queen Mary holds in the affection and confidence of the Hong Kong Chinese).

What could I do for him that had not already been done, for he had been through some of the most august medical hands in the Colony? But I prayed with and for him. He said he did not understand what prayer signified. I explained what it meant and to whom we were praying. (I usually stress, " If ye ask anything in My Name. . .")

In two days my countryman came back and said he was well. This is a commonplace in the remissions of peptic ulceration and so I comforted him and gave him further medicine with prayer and advice, not at all believing that it was as he said. Toward the end of the week he was back again and this time he was adamant—he would take no more medicine.

This incident happened three years ago and only once has he come back for medical advice; not infrequently I have seen him casually and on one occasion I have preached in the chapel he has set up in his village. For he went home to his village, and his enthusiastic testimony was sufficient to make all his friends and relatives burn their idols. They all turned to the Lord and believed.

The continuation of the story is that there is now a well-attended church in the village, and Lutheran World Service is building a clinic there right next to the Chinese border, which is the Bamboo Curtain.

Chapter Six

Some Experiences with the Communists

W E KNOW SOMETHING ABOUT COMMUNISM! WHAT HOPE is there from such a system? Think of the cruelty and brutality of Communism, and the notorious village trials, when mob passion is made the pawn of the judge. An accused person has little hope of anything but death by one of their four methods: being buried alive; being repeatedly dropped from a height of about fifteen feet; being dragged by an arm or a leg by a galloping horse until pulled to pieces; being beaten to death. This is devilish, but horrible to relate the judges are sincere. What terror to fall into the hands of these callow youths, most of whom are quite uneducated!

A district coroner brought me part of a sheep's head and a bone from a sheep's leg, and asked me if these were human remains. He had, he said, a man under suspicion of murder, and these bones were part of the evidence against him. Poor accused! I wondered what was the other part of the evidence and what were the ulterior motives. The coroner was not convinced by my statements, so I suggested to Dr. Bessie that we show him the illustrations in Cunningham's *Anatomy*. "I beg of you not to," she said. "He has never seen such a book, and will immediately borrow it, and that is the last we will see of it."

Another of these youths corrected my knowledge of Australia, first by making the most outlandish and unbelievable corrections, and then telling me straight out that I was ignorant and didn't know.

No series of descriptions of treatment by people who have passed through Communist hands are alike except in this—

that they contradict one another.

Take a few personal experiences. The China Inland Mission hospital in Kaifeng was treated very reasonably, while the Seventh Day Adventist hospital in a nearby town was looted and burned to the ground. Thus force was used in the one case and gradual infiltration in the other. This infiltration of the C.I.M. hospital was a gradual process, which we were very slow to recognize. In 1948 Mr. Liu the Chinese business manager, was taken off for indoctrination. His later report showed that missionary work in China would soon be at an end, but at that time the missionaries were still being treated reasonably. When Mr. Liu and Elder Kung told us that soon there would not be a missionary left in China, there were very few missionaries who were inclined to believe them. One of our number even said they were maligning the Communists. " I've been in their hands and they are not bad at all," said he. Events have proved them worse than our blackest pessimist predicted. I myself was not badly treated by them—the Japanese were far worse—yet others have been beaten to death.

Dr. Li, the Chinese medical superintendent of the C.I.M. hospital, and the lady almoner were both taken off for interrogation. Neither of them fully recovered, and Dr. Li died shortly afterward from treatment received. This was quite simple. Each of them was made to sit in a chair for a month. Effective cruelty! At the end of the time neither of them could walk, and both were dropsical.

Terms such as religious liberty, true democracy, women's rights, no censorship, and so on are on everybody's lips and painted on every wall. But China and Russia have never known democracy. They have no conception of what we mean by the freedom of the individual. The country Chinese accept what is given them; their highest wish is peace and enough food to keep alive.

Censorship in our sense is not needed. The atmosphere is so electric with spying, that everyone is on guard. The situation is exactly adumbrated in the Minor Prophets:

A PEKING CART

"Trust ye not in a friend, put ye not confidence in a guide : keep the door of thy mouth from her that lieth in thy bosom " (Mic. 7 : 5).

"Religious liberty " is in banner headlines in every village. Yet it would be as much as one's life is worth to attempt to preach. The words, "True Democracy," are printed everywhere, but there is only one candidate, one party, and one square for your vote. Stalin declared that they alone have true democracy.

About July, 1949, I applied for a Communist pass out of China. After four months of anxiety and hope deferred, three secret police came to say that it had been granted. "But we wish first to examine your political opinions. You might, of course, easily be a spy. We want to find out all about you, and so tomorrow three commissars will examine you. You have nothing to fear. You will not be confined, nor detained, but will be allowed back to your friends almost immediately." This, and a lot more like it was said, and I began to get ready for the worst. I did not feel at all like an innocent man on a routine application for a pass.

The next day Heng-shin and I set out for the first Communist commissar in a Peking cart, drawn by a beautiful mule. On arrival, we found the youthful commissar and his companions at breakfast. No bourgeois manners for them! They were all squatting on the floor eating. They took scant notice of me and my companion. When they had finished their leader motioned us to follow him. His office was dressed with a red flag and a high seat for my questioning. The high seat was his! On my left sat three young men on a bed. They were the commissar's assistants; on my right lay a wounded Communist soldier.

The commissar first asked what were the relative distances of England and Australia from China. I had used a hearing aid for some years. I thought it wise to leave this in the cart outside the village. He therefore had to leave his "throne " and shout in my ear. If my answers did not satisfy him, he simply contradicted me and told me I did not know. He did this when I said Australians spoke English, and pitied my

ignorance when I said Australia, a continent, did not contain many countries like Asia. I knew that all this was but
preliminary jockeying for the right atmosphere.

Suddenly he paused, and I sensed the crisis coming. He
came closer and shouted, " Do you love us?" To reply in
the negative was impossible; it would probably have cost
both our lives. On the other hand, a simple " Yes " was also

impossible. I said, "Eh?" Then before he could repeat the question, I said, "Your voice is very hoarse." This produced an unexpected reaction. His three assistants, who had been silent so far, suddenly found their voices.

"He is our political speaker, and we are afraid he will lose his voice. Can you do anything for him, Doctor?" one of them said. I immediately saw this as my way of escape and gave the young commissar the most thorough overhaul possible.

After about an hour of my pummelling and questioning—I went thoroughly into his family history—he suddenly looked at his watch. "Why our time is gone," he said, "I must write my report, and send you on to the next commissar." I prescribed for him and he was more than satisfied. Then he sat down to write. Not one political question had he asked me. As China is constituted, there was no difficulty in Heng-shin's looking over the young man's shoulder as he was writing. Heng-shin is a Chinese scholar, the communist wasn't. At first Heng-shin only corrected the commissar's "white characters." A "white character" is a sure sign in China of lack of education; it is one with a similar sound but different meaning. Then later he began to correct the grammar and style. For this the Communist was truly grateful. Suddenly, much to my delight, he handed over pen and paper to Heng-shin. I noticed that Heng-shin continued with a brush, which few of the modern Communists can use. I was in no way responsible for what he wrote, but his report took me through the next two commissars with scarcely any further questioning. On my arrival in Shanghai, it was almost immediately instrumental in procuring me a pass out of China.

The third and last commissar lived in Taian, near the famous Confucian mountain of Tai-shan. When eventually, I stood before him, he took no notice of me, but continued reading a brochure in which he was engrossed.

My report was on the table beside him—apparently he had already read it. Suddenly he looked up and said to Heng-shin, "This is not what I wanted to know, but for all that it is very interesting. I asked you for a statement of your numbers, your organization, and your distribution, but you have given me a testimony."

Heng-shin answered, " Our numbers we do not know. We are growing like the seed planted in the earth, we know not how. Our beliefs and organization are all in this book," and he drew a Bible out of his pocket. " As to our distribution, we stretch all across North China."

The commissar said nothing, but turning to me he apparently recollected that it was with me that he had to do, for he said, " Your pass is granted, and you must leave for Shanghai tomorrow night."

" Could I not go to Tientsin?" I said, " Shanghai is blockaded, and it may be impossible to leave China from that port."

" Of course, I will give you a pass to Tientsin. On arrival there you will be met by the police, who, on my authority, will give you a pass to Peking. In Peking you will see the chief commissar of all China, who alone can give you a pass on a ship leaving Tientsin. But you will go to Shanghai tomorrow night."

Nonplussed I said again, " But I do not want to go to Shanghai; it is blockaded. I would rather go to Tientsin."

" Of course," he replied, and repeated what he had just said word for word, ending as before with, " But you will go to Shanghai tomorrow night." What more adequate method for bewildering one could have been thought of? Logical thought and language itself become useless. For the first time I realized that drugs were not necessary thoroughly to confuse and bamboozle a person.

The commissar went on, " We have prepared a place for you in the jail. You cannot leave the city tonight."

This made me really tremble; anyone who has seen a Chinese jail knows why. Another of the remarkable occurrences of that remarkable day then happened.

The commissar turned again to his brochure. Some Chinese standing at the door beckoned. Immediately I was in the cart and was soon outside the city gates on the way to Tai-shan. No one was more astounded than I. Why had he allowed me to go? Every moment I expected to be followed and brought back. Nothing happened, and soon night descended. We took a side track and began to ascend. Lights and lanterns appeared, and on all sides there were shouts and laughter and cries of welcome. We had reached another Home of Jesus, this one on Tai-shan itself.

A few years before, on the mountain spur, the Japanese had been preparing gun emplacements for the protection of the railway yards down in the valley. An immense amount of grading, road building, and rock work had been done, and all this fell into the hands of these Christians of this Home of Jesus. They had done wonders, and were transforming this wilderness into a paradise.

On this mountain they had five establishments, for farming, orchards, dairying, sheepfolds, and piggeries. Never was there a more interesting and delightful place. The chapel of hewn stone was nearing completion. Their stonework was good, and they had abundant supplies "presented" to them by the Japanese!

After the anxieties and fatigues of the day, we had the most loving of Christian welcomes. A bath and change prepared me for such a meal as only rural China can produce, flavours that our "gross and uneducated palates" cannot appreciate, sea foods and fish that we do not know exist.

During this love-feast I said to the pastor, "The commissar says that I must leave for Shanghai tomorrow night."

"That is unfortunate," he said, "we just happen to be out of money; thus there is none for your ticket."

I thought of the beautiful mule that had drawn our cart that day; not long before they had paid $200.00 gold for it. I thought to myself that these people must be living literally from hand to mouth. It was so, as the sequel proved.

The pastor immediately formed two plans for getting the money. Two train tickets would be necessary, for they were sending Heng-shin with me. By next morning the two plans had come to naught. These were the plans. "Catch the night train," he said to Mr. Ting-shui-chi, the treasurer, "go to our brethren in Tsinan: perhaps they can give us the money." Then he said to Mr. Chow, a deacon, " Go tomorrow morning and ask the commissar for a day of grace." The night train was crowded, and Mr. Ting could not buy a ticket. The commissar sneered at Mr. Chow. He would not believe that the foreigner did not have enough money for his train fare, so Mr. Chow reported that there must be no change of plans. " Here's an impasse," I thought. " What will they do now?" I was in their hands, and they had assumed full responsibility. What a wonderful position for a missionary to be in!

The pastor's way out of the difficulty was to call us to prayer. There were about twelve Chinese and two foreigners at his prayer meeting, for Miss Syltevik, a Norwegian lady, was staying there at that time.

" Can God spread a table in the wilderness? This must prove to be a case of Elijah and the ravens," I thought. Our little community was isolated on the mountain, not a soul lived near. There could be no expectation or prospect of getting anything. Yes, I was very doubtful, and when I went out I looked up into the sky to see if haply there might be ravens about.

Afar off down in the valley I could see the road from Peking and the North, but in these disturbed days there was little traffic on it. I continued my walk in the orchard. About noon I returned and was met by Helen Tso. " We have the money for your two tickets, elder brother," she called out. She introduced me to a young Chinese, whom I had not seen before, and said, " He brought it."

As far as I could gather, the story was this. He had left Peking two days before, and on the road below, just out of sight, his bus had broken down. From below he could see this place as a green patch on the mountain. He wondered what it was and climbed to investigate. " When he saw the chapel and surroundings, he was so impressed that he gave us this, and it is just enough for your two third-class tickets to Shanghai." And that is the story of how I said good-bye to the Ye-Su Chia-ting in Shantung.

The train was late and crowded that night. For two days and nights Heng-shin and I sat cooped up and crowded. We dozed and talked, and looked at the passing scene. Two things we noticed particularly: the crowded, closed troop trains, and the myriads of men, women, and even children, doing forced labour on the ruined bridges and railway lines. This was in November, 1949. Often since I have wondered about those crowded troop trains. Why were they hurrying North? Was Korea in mind even then? That was nine or ten months before the trouble there actually started.

Chapter Seven

The Indigenous Church

MY ARRIVAL FOR THE FIRST TIME IN CHINA IN 1921 almost coincided with the beginning of the two largest indigenous church movements in that country. The former was the Ye-Su Chia-ting; the latter is oftenest called The Little Flock. It is a very heartening fact that both these movements, which began independently of one another, owe their genesis to two foreign ladies.

Miss Barbour, an English worker with the Church Missionary Society was the force behind Mr. Watchman Nee, the founder of The Little Flock movement. Miss Dillenbeck of the American Methodists had great influence on Mr. Ching, the founder of the Ye-Su Chia-ting. Her grave is in Ma-Chuang, which she helped to establish and to which she gave her life.

From the early 20's, missionaries began to see with increasing clarity the necessity for the establishment of Chinese churches which were independent of foreign support. How frequently I heard Mr. Gibb, the General Director of the China Inland Mission, say, " A foreigner cannot be the pastor of a Chinese church." In 1928, Mr. Gibb undertook a world tour, and everywhere at missionary conferences he expressed this view and the new policy of the C.I.M. to establish indigenous Chinese churches. " All church control," he said, " must pass to Chinese leaders." Thank God, from that time on the C.I.M. rigorously pursued this policy, and so did other missionary societies. If this had not been so, how doubly hopeless had the present situation been.

A young commissar told me that, in his opinion, the Chinese church was a foreign thing. It only carried on because of foreign help. Remove this help, and the supposed church would collapse, without any policy or effort on the part of the Communists themselves. How nearly right he was!

The Roman church, of all that claim to be Christian, has been swept away most completely by the Communists. It is instructive to take a glance at the Romanists. There is no such thing as the indigenous principle in their dealings with native churches. How then do they maintain themselves? The force principle enters very largely into their theological philosophy. Their vows, their obedience, their submission, and so on, bind them with iron chains, not to God the Father and His Son our Lord Jesus Christ, but to a centralized hierarchy, which is their final standard and court of appeal.

Communists fear the Roman system because they understand it. They are utterly at a loss when they meet the Ye-Su Chia-ting. Their puerile accusations against it prove their bewilderment.

It is not so with their accusations against Rome, which they all believe. Are they true? I want to deal with some of them, because of the light they throw on this problem of the indigenous church and its relationship to the Communists.

While I was in hospital in Tsinan under Communist control, the Communists permitted Roman Catholic priests, two at a time, to pay visits. Among other things they said, "Christianity is finished in North China," and then they revealed the havoc which had been wrought among the Roman Catholics. I was not ignorant of this, but how delighted I was to tell them they could set their hearts at rest, for Christianity had not been wiped out. I had just been at a conference at which there were seventy Chinese leaders from Shantung alone. Their system was so foreign to the indigenous church idea that I could see they completely failed to comprehend me. That they did not believe me is not relevant. They could understand neither my words nor what was happening.

The Roman Catholic mind has a very terrible twist, which has been mentioned by Lord Hatherley, who writes of men "imbued with the deadly taint of Romanism." "I mean," he says, "that poison which perverts the uprightness and candour of the mind, and allows people to think themselves honest, when they are speaking only half their real thought, and then in such a way as to mislead those who are not aware of their concealed purpose."

Take this as an illustration. I quote from a passage taken from a French publication (*Annales de la Propagation de la Foi* 238): "This house has already this year received four hundred and ninety-two children, and three hundred and fifty-six have already flown to Heaven immediately after their baptism. Out of more than twelve thousand baptized in this orphan establishment . . . not more than one hundred and twenty-four or one hundred and twenty-five lived more than a year."

These statements, made so naïvely, are without a suspicion of evil, and show how grievously tainted is Roman mission work. When I read this I was truly startled, because it is one of their own statements, not a piece of Communist propaganda. My Chinese friends all know this, and they commonly accuse the Roman Catholic orphanages of taking no care at all of the children because of their twisted beliefs in baptismal regeneration. But the Roman Catholics think they are unjustly condemned. The same holds true of their enormous land holdings in China, but I need not pursue the subject further.

The Communists have made use of all these things against the indigenous church. "This is Christianity," they say. Only God-given wisdom has guided the Christians through these shoals. I have touched only the fringe of what the Chinese know and fear about what is called "foreign mission work." I have been describing what a Roman Catholic non-indigenous church is like. This is the antithesis of true apostolic work.

The Communist hope that the church would collapse has not materialized, as is shown by the various shifts they have used for controlling church organization. The "Plenary" conference of church leaders in 1949 in Peking, although claiming to be representative, was, of course, not so. How easy it is for the Communists to get control of anything that is organized on human lines, an organization, not an organism. It is very remarkable that the very weakness of Protestantism is its strength. A subversive power cannot undermine its local autonomy or its individuality. And this is so with the indigenous churches in China.

In the last chapter I mentioned the question put by the Communist commissar in Taian to Heng-shin "I want a statement of your numbers, your distribution, and your organization."

It was easy for him to give a completely evasive but quite truthful reply. When the centre of control of a number of churches is in Heaven, what can the Communists do? But when it is on earth what can they not do? This is the position. The Communists cannot put a subverter in every tiny village church, but they only need one for a centralized organization—and how easily the churches are controlled, and that through their own machinery!

The leader of The Little Flock told me that groups of their churches carried on all over Manchuria during the Japanese occupation, wholly untouched by attempts at Japanese control. On the other hand, churches much larger in number, but with a centralized control like most of our home churches, were controlled from the outset by a Japanese oligarchy.

How difficult the Communists will find the problem of controlling the numbers of hidden, small, and scattered Chia-ting churches! They have no central organization; their only bond is the love and fear of God, and their worship of the Trinity.

Frequently there are no church buildings, and there is no doubt that in the present circumstances, fewer and fewer special buildings will be put up. Many groups meet only in Chinese houses. The only officials in the local churches are elders and deacons.

I heard of a communion service, told by the one who led it, in a long-established Communist area. An elder and a deacon officiated. The communicants came singly, in order, but not in a pre-arranged order, simply by watching and going after the last had left. Thus three were present each time; they prayed and wept together, the narrator said, and then partook of the elements.

Just before I arrived in MaChuang, Shantung had passed through a very severe famine. Money was pouring in from abroad, especially from the U.S.A., so that by the time I reached MaChuang, conditions had almost returned to normal. What rather amazed me was that the Chia-ting churches would not touch any of this money. The wisdom of this did not appear until the Communists had full power in 1949. Then they minutely went through all accounts, and found what moneys had been received from abroad. Any church in receipt of foreign funds was liquidated. It mattered not at what time nor for what purpose those funds had been given.

Mr. Ching had just received a letter from a group of churches in America. He showed it to me when I arrived. If the Chia-ting churches would take the name of this foreign group, then this group of churches would assume all the Chia-ting financial responsibilities. It was a kindly act—"No more financial worries."

But Mr. Ching's attitude was different. He said, "They do not know our spirit. Those foreign churches would rob us of one of our sheet anchors. It is our financial need which drives us to our knees, and forces us to cry unto Him."

I met this attitude in action again later on. In July, 1949, I attended a meeting of more than 120 leaders of these churches. One of the subjects on the agenda was the financial help needed by lately opened churches. This caused much discussion and prayer. They reviewed all the way along which they had come, and the great question at issue was, would they rob these churches of spiritual experience by giving them another source of supply, which might not be direct from God? The New Testament attitude and St. Paul's statements were fully brought under review.

A body of believers is tested and proved by their relation to finance, and in this matter these churches constantly sought God's face. "There is a reason," they said, "why finance is so little mentioned in the Acts, although St. Paul must have needed much money on his travels. Who can uncover the mighty acts of God so peculiar and so individually precious!"

Mr. Baller of the C.I.M. used to say that the Chinese character shows two extremes. If the rest of their nation has often shown corruption in money matters, then these Christians have arrived at a wonderful financial maturity.

Mr. Hoste of the C.I.M. often said to me, "Remember, Doctor, the Chinese are an imperial people." In many spheres of human endeavour, the Chinese actually have great cause for complacency.

The ethical and philosophical systems of Confucius and Mencius adumbrate much that is best in Western thought, while such thinkers as Chuang-Tzi and Men-Tzi contain thoughts so surprisingly modern that they might be culled from Einstein or Marx. Truly their land is favoured; its rivers, its mountains, its natural products and scenery astonish Western travellers. Where the Chinese fall short is in human relationships, in integrity, and in mutual help. These Chinese Christians recognize the shortcomings of their nation, and God has enlightened their eyes to see the Fountain whence these things come.

Sun-Yat-Sen called his countrymen, "A plate of sand." There can be in a nation or group of people either one of two cementing links; love and integrity on the one hand, or force and dictatorship on the other. The Chinese have been forced to submit to the latter, and one of the most significant events in history has taken place; the mission church has been forced out of China. Either directly or indirectly as a result of foreign missionary work, an indigenous Chinese church is left to be a witness in the midst of Communism. Therefore we can praise God and take courage.

I have been asked not infrequently, "How can an indigenous church be brought into being?" or "How is one to recognize an indigenous church?" I can only say, "The kingdom of God cometh not with observation: neither shall they say, Lo here! or, lo there! Suddenly one is conscious that it is in our midst. It is like the seed that a man cast into the ground. Day and night he observed and watched it; but it grew he knew not how."

The Communists have the impression that the church is something foreign by nature. "Restrict preaching and this exotic thing will soon die out," say they. To their astonishment they find something in their midst that is not in the least foreign. It is in its essence Chinese, and they cannot deny it. It is so essentially so in all its " flavours and colours " that they cannot but recognize it as theirs.

Frequently we missionaries are so foreign and insular, that we imagine our own type of Christianity to be the only legitimate variety. How difficult it is for us to be Chinese or Indians or Africans. Yet we must truly endeavour to harmonize very closely with them, if we are to have true fellowship with those whom God has converted through our ministry. These things being so, it is not to be wondered at that many missionary societies did not recognize the local churches that had sprung up in their midst. Naturally, it is difficult to recognize something so entirely new as an indigenous movement can be.

Let me instance the united praying aloud of all the individuals in a congregation. To our ears the noise is tremendous and most distracting. But this is just what the Chinese like. They have it in their schools, and it has advantages. " It is not distracting to God," they say, " and look how it encourages the timid ones." These suddenly burst out into prayer, when they have never prayed before.

Take the case of Chinese hymns. Most of the hymns in foreign mission hymnbooks are translations, often by foreigners. We missionaries sing them with easy understanding; we have sung them in our own language from our youth up. But what of the Chinese? How, for instance, does a new convert get on with the translation of "Rock of Ages," and many other similar foreign conceptions?

No doubt he understands them later on, but a heathen

Chinese gets a very doubtful impression, so different from what he gets when he looks into one of their very own hymnbooks.

Let us look at one belonging to a local native church. We notice immediately how different it is. The style is different. It is a style of Chinese with which a missionary often does not become familiar. Three or four thousand years of history produce many styles. It is abbreviated, classical, and often has no rhyme. The thought is Chinese and may be very idomatic, topical, and local. It is sometimes incomprehensible to us, yet it is very precious to the Chinese who sing it. How would you enjoy a service in which most of the congregation know the hymnbook and the Psalms by heart? Let us sing Psalm 84, or 100, or 38, as the case might be. Voices are immediately raised with very few in the congregation looking at a book. Frequently the song leader does not even announce the number of a hymn, and it is sung as we sing a chorus, although there may be many verses in it. "Let us sing First Corinthians, chapter 13," says the preacher, and without hesitation the congregation sings.

How would you like to sit through a meeting which began at 6 p.m., and ended at 5 a.m. the next morning? Almost the whole of the meeting was taken up with testimonies, and comments by the chairman or pastor. No-one who testified was limited in time and no-one was bored. The congregation finishes these long, long services refreshed and full of enthusiasm. I have said "long, long," because that is how they seemed to me. The Chinese considered that this was my foreignness, and since they are the important ones, it is I who must change my point of view, not they.

The indigenous church is in a position to react in a wonderful way to its foreign friends. These dear brethren faced death for me, and when the Communists called me for an interview, I was never alone. When I travelled I always had companionship, somebody to ease the toils and broils, and those who have travelled in China will know what I mean by this. How often I have heard Mr. Hoste of the C.I.M., praying for a party setting out for the interior, say, "And protect them,

Lord, from unreasonable and wicked men." Travel in China makes these toils and difficulties very great.

Never shall I forget what Heng-shin did for me, when we were interned by the Japanese. He came through the Japanese guards, while Dr. Harry Taylor and I were shut up, and brought us quite a large gift of money. This came from the Chia-ting churches in North China, just when we had no money. The Japanese, though keeping us interned, made us supply our own needs.

Once, while I was staying in MaChuang, I complained about one of the brethren to Heng-shin. "Do you know," he said, "that that brother would lay down his life for you!" It was not long before this brother gave me the opportunity to know that it was so. That was the end of my complaints.

The relation between a foreign missionary and an indigenous church must of necessity be different from the usual missionary relationship, even though the missionary was the instrument raised up by God to bring that church into being. It is so easy for a missionary to take a position which is artificial and which depends on his foreign prestige.

The missionary movement and the indigenous movement are bound together in the bonds of life. It is for the missionary to be in constant prayer and humility, that leaders in the native churches may be recognized and given their rightful authority. The missionary must be careful to place himself in the background. The native church will see that he does not remain there long, if he is worthy.

The fruits borne by the indigenous church will be immediately and constantly seen in the amelioration of the whole social structure of the surrounding country. It is a truism that it is not laws that are needed in a land, but good citizens who will obey the laws, those who fear God and keep His commandments.

All around the Homes of the Christians the roads, the bridges and the public services are good. They are constantly kept in repair without any sign from the government. Our roads, our bridges, our public amenities, all depend upon public morality. Why do such amenities as bridges soon disappear from country rivers in East Asia? Simply because of the beachcombing tendencies of the local people, who steal the wood and iron contained therein. The most beautiful buildings are soon destroyed by looters.

Famine relief was poured into China, bridges were built on the roads in the North-West. Why is not a vestige left? Why do the officials line their own pockets? If we do not do these things too, it is not because of the greater efficacy of our laws, but simply because there are more lawkeepers in other words, more " salt," to use our Lord's words. All around the Chia-ting settlements roads are improved, bridges are built and kept in repair, the breeding of cattle is studied, and crops improved. There is an eagerness to learn, an enterprising spirit. When his incubators were full and he still had more eggs for hatching, Ru-Shun climbed the trees at the back and placed an egg in each rook's nest, and he lost very few. When they couldn't procure petrol, they worked for three days on one of their big engines and made it go on charcoal gas. When they found I didn't have a pocket-knife, one of the boys made me one, which I still use.

To the Communists, Sunday as a day of rest is illegal. Yet these Christians carry on their services as usual. They do it by means of sending out working parties to help anyone who is in need in the district. The services are held when they are off duty, and the Communists know this. It needs no one to tell you which are Chia-ting fields, just as a smiling, healthy Chia-ting face can be distinguished in a crowd. And all this flows from one Source only.

They honour, fear and love God. They honour the Son even as they honour the Father. They believe, with the Nicean Creed, that the Holy Spirit is the Lord and Giver of life, who with the Father and Son together, is to be worshipped and glorified. The Scriptures are their final court of appeal, and they take them literally. When seeing some of the things they do, I could not but glorify God in them. I found myself saying with a catch in my voice, " Why, *all* the Bible is true; I have only believed it in theory up till now."

A Sequel

In 1952 my wife and I decided that the time had arrived for us to return to our missionary calling. I was doing the work of a ship's surgeon and my ship was in Melbourne. I had just enough money to take me to Borneo.

Unknown to me, but with the same urge to preach to the Chinese in the islands of S.E. Asia, was the Rev. John Chen, trained in the China Inland Mission Changsha Bible Institute. He had left Hong Kong on a temporary pass, and we arrived almost simultaneously in Labuan, the island off North Borneo on which the air-strip is. It was Sunday morning and we met in the little Church of England Chinese church. In this church there was a very faithful lay reader, Mr. C. T. Liang. We discussed with him how best the Chinese workers, rubber planters and traders could be reached. They live mostly on the numerous rivers which flow from central Borneo, like the irregular spokes of a huge wheel.

We mapped out our itinerary and began. In the two months allowed by John Chen's pass we gathered together a handful of Chinese believers at a little place called Lawas (nearby is the headquarters station of the Borneo Evangelical Mission, which ministers to the native Dyaks and Malays).

Little knowing what the future held, this little handful were left to their own devices, while John and I returned to our homelands, I to England, John to China. We had planned a concerted attack upon the Chinese of North Borneo. I returned in 1955 to Hong Kong with the object of helping John get a passport to Borneo. Time passed rapidly. Various objections were raised by the authorities and John's passport was held up. We mourned about the few believers; how we wanted to help them, and establish, as we imagined, a strong Chinese church. While we waited in Hong Kong I opened two clinics there. It became obvious after waiting two years that it was doubtful whether the British authorities would allow John Chen or any other Chinese into Sarawak or North Borneo. I am afraid we gave up hope and, of course, thought that without our help our few Chinese believers would by now be scattered; the little work we had done was worthless and finished. But why? Had we not begun as an act of faith? Did not St. Paul do work in this way?

I thought of the believers at Derbe and Lystra. How long did Paul and Barnabas work among them? How soon the two apostles passed on, and when they left, far from the believers begging them to stay and build a church-building there, on the contrary they were filled with joy and the Holy Ghost at their departure. Why did not this happen to us? Why did it not happen as I had seen it happen in North China, while I was with the Ye-Su Chia-ting? Why did it not happen? But it did.

In November, 1956, I received a letter from the Chairman of the Borneo Evangelical Mission at Lawas. He wrote, "We now have here a Chinese church of more than thirty believers, meeting regularly and managing all their own affairs".

How had God wrought in our absence, and how contrary to all our expectations, exceeding abundantly above all we asked or thought! How John and I bless God that we could not return, or we might have spoiled the work of God!

I knew all this in theory; I knew that believers must be left to the Holy Spirit, if they are to grow, but still *we* wanted to do it and take the place of the Holy Spirit, "It is God that worketh in us both to will and do of His good pleasure." So here is the answer to those who have asked me: "How to preach that an indigenous church may be formed."

Here is a church which knows nothing of foreign money, but needs the help that St. Paul gave of prayer and written epistles. Mr. Belcher also adds that the faithful Mr. Liang, the lay reader from Labuan, also goes across on occasion to minister to them. This is necessary, as his is the Chinese dialect that is common in the district.

Thus by following apostolic example the establishment of an indigenous church is still possible to us missionaries at this point in world and church history. May it become a common practice, a normal missionary operation.